HAYES PRESS

The Battle

An Anthology of Spiritual Warfare – Volume 1

HAYES
PRESS Christian Publisher

Published by: Hayes Press, The Barn, Flaxlands, Royal Wootton Bassett, Swindon, United Kingdom, SN4 8DY. t. +44 (0) 1793 850958 e. info@hayespress.org www.facebook.com/hayespress.org

First edition

This book was professionally typeset on Reedsy.
Find out more at reedsy.com

To all those who have fought the good fight ahead of us and lived lives worthy of their calling, inspiring us to do likewise. To our fellow-soldiers around the world, each fighting their own daily battles on the Lord's side – may this book help strengthen our hands in God. Above all, to God our Saviour and His Son, Jesus Christ, Who give us the victory!

Contents

Acknowledgement

We would like to sincerely acknowledge the many people who have helped to bring this project to fruition. The YFR Committee supported this vision wholeheartedly from the beginning, which was a great encouragement. David Webster ably reviewed the book for content and provided some helpful suggestions. Jennifer Jones proof-read and Ade Kukoyi (www.kukisart.com) designed the book cover. Kevin Hickling at Hayes Press (www.hayespress.org) has been very supportive behind the scenes, particularly in terms of publishing, marketing and distribution support. Finally, to our contributors, without whom most of the content would not have existed. We hope that you enjoy reading it and are blessed by it.

1 OOHRAH! (JON NEELY)

War. It has been a part of human history since the very beginning and though we may not play a direct role ourselves, we're all aware of the impact it has on the world we live in. War is real and affects the lives of millions around the world.

In the United States it is no different. The Army, the Navy and the Marines are, among others, major factors in the proceedings both on their own soil and on the ground, air, and sea in nations spanning the globe. Though much is kept from civilians, there are still familiar sounds and images of war that resonate through our minds, whether seen live or portrayed through film; some of brutality, some of hope, all feeling very distant from here. One common military saying in particular is recognizable to many and bares much significance and importance to those who voice it: "OohRah."

It is a term, used by Marines, that may not have a definite spelling or concrete pronunciation (depending on the section of military you are from), but its importance is never questioned. "OohRah"; a phrase that signifies the willingness and readiness for battle; that those who shout it are highly trained to diligently follow those in charge, focused on the task at hand. They are prepared. It is a phrase that signifies a warrior.

To those of us who don't live a daily life surrounded by war, we hear this and it seems millions of miles away. We have no plans to see it up close. We have confidence that our enemies are far away and that those who have the job of protecting us will do so. No need for us to lift a finger. We live our lives - Christian or otherwise - in a place that offers much opportunity; where God's beauty is constantly on display. There is no war-like danger - everything is just fine. No need for "OohRah" here. This is how we feel and we are terribly, terribly mistaken.

"Be alert....Your enemy the devil prowls around like a roaring lion looking for someone to devour" (1 Peter 5:8).

Is that what you see here? Those deceitful eyes of the enemy glaring through the beauty; waiting ever so patiently to devour? The verse is a warning primarily pertaining to overseers, but it is clearly a general caution to us all. This is not a danger that lingers in a far-off land. This danger is as up close and personal as it gets.

As Christians we are often reminded of God's beauty and wonder as we survey His wondrous creation around us. We are taught of His love and compassion from Sunday school on up. It is all good and true, but do we take notice of what else is happening? That amidst this world of beauty and opportunity there is an event of tremendous importance taking place: We are at war.

Never more has a statement been so authentic and so urgent. It is the most dangerous and important war this world will ever see, which is why it is so shocking that we act like nothing is happening. We live our lives and focus on the good; the birds singing, the sun shining, the latest Twilight Saga movie to come out. We hear of wars in other countries and we escape them by simply changing the channel. If the biggest concern of a war we have is supporting our troops overseas, then we are missing the point entirely, and putting ourselves at risk. We are crazy to think the war is anywhere else but right here, right now. When we act like it is not right on top of us, we fool ourselves and thus we open our hearts to the deception of the prowling lion, waiting in the weeds to pounce on his unsuspecting prey.

Maybe we forget about the raging war because we already know who is victorious. Those who choose to follow Christ will one day leave this sin-stricken world and spend eternity by His side. This is not gym class, where the teams are chosen first and then the battle is decided. No, we are well aware that the winner is already declared in this war. Christ came down and, with one humanity-saving knockout punch to all that is evil, won the battle - leaving Him bruised and bloodied for us, by us.

With Him, our battle is won, yet if our inclination is that the risk is gone, then we are fooling ourselves; blind to an evil power intertwined in this world that cannot be ignored. If you are going to be a member of this team, if you are going to choose the winning side, then you are a part of something much bigger than yourself, and you have a crucial role in this endeavour - now, more than ever.

Maybe we do not see the war at hand because we are not forced to watch in horror as explosions fill the sky above us, forced to cover our ears as gunfire echoes through the night, or hurriedly step aside as armoured vehicles thunder past. All that would suggest to us that we are a part of such a war. We would certainly guard ourselves if bullets were flying overhead at the dinner table. Check, please. Without all that, though, we are unperceptive to the real action. We do not see such things because this is not a war fought with guns and planes; they pale in comparison to the power at hand. No nuclear weapon could come close to the forces at display in this war. Sure, they may play a part, but this is a clash of much, much more. This is good vs. evil; a phrase we dabble with jokingly, but one that should send a shiver down our spine. Our enemy is the most formidable opponent in history and it is us whom he seeks to destroy. If we are missing the big picture here

-that war is upon us - then we are in more trouble than we think.

The medieval author Thomas à Kempis once warned, "the devil sleepeth not, neither is the flesh as yet dead; therefore cease not to prepare thyself for the battle, for on the right hand and on the left are enemies who never rest." The truth is chilling: the enemy never sleeps. We are up against one who is both like a roaring lion and one who "masquerades as an angel of light" (2 Corinthians 11:14). This is not the bearded lunatic at the corner chanting "the end is near." The evil we are opposing is immense. This is real life and death. This is spiritual warfare, and it is not to be taken lightly. The world tells us to concern ourselves with trivial matters. The news begins every night with urgent updates pertaining to strikes, scandals and sinking ships. Celebrities fill our screens demanding we change our lifestyles and "go green," focusing on the damage we are doing to the earth. "Use these light bulbs!" "Buy this car!" "Check out how earth-aware we are!" This is the modern day version of doing good in the world. Plant a tree and we can sleep soundly at night. If this is where our focus is, it will be our downfall. Do not put importance on unimportant world issues. In the end, the Lord decides when to destroy the world and rid it of sin. He will do it effortlessly and with purpose. The world became sick with the bite of a forbidden fruit; whether or not you recycle has little consequence.

It is just one of many examples that the world tells us to worry about, but the world is dead wrong. We need to be aware of the pivotal conflict we are a part of and concentrate on the roles we have been given by God. This is where our primary focus should be. We cannot hide on the sidelines.

The devil is sinister in all his ways. Sin is not the only way he gains the upper hand in our lives. If he sways our focus from Christ - whether we are looking at pop cans or pornography - he is getting his way. Sounds crazy, but the devil does not need us to bite the hand that feeds us. He just needs us to look for food elsewhere. If we are not doing what God wants us to do - no matter how we fill our time - is God getting any glory from us? Are we useful to Him at all?

The evening news ought not to start with global warming, but rather, a global warning. A warning of what truly is the most urgent matter - that we are in grave danger if we are not preparing ourselves daily; a warning about all the power and deception that the devil is playing with - and he knows he has but a short time left (Revelation 12:12).

"...be strong in the Lord and in his mighty power. Put on the full armour of God, so that you can take your stand against the devil's schemes. For our struggle is not against flesh and blood, but against the rulers, against the authorities, against the powers of this dark world and against the spiritual forces of evil in the heavenly realms" (Ephesians 6:10-12).

If it is a news break we are looking for, we ought to try this one: the biggest issue in the world is the world itself, and the spiritual forces of evil that are at work. This, friends, is as real as it gets. This isn't a decree for us to throw out our belongings, unplug ourselves from social media and find a nice, empty field to set up a tent in and call home. This doesn't mean we cannot enjoy aspects of this world - it would be a waste not to go and live our lives to the full. This is a call to recognize what is transpiring and not only pay attention to its importance, but pay the price for it – just as Christ did.

"Therefore, I urge you, brothers and sisters, in view of God's mercy, to offer your bodies as a living sacrifice, holy and pleasing to God - this is your true and proper worship. Do not conform to the pattern of this world, but be transformed by the renewing of your mind. Then you will be able to test and approve what God's will is - his good, pleasing and perfect will" (Romans 12:1-2).

When we concern ourselves with the Lord's things and all He has to offer, we are not succumbing to a life of required boredom and incessant slow-moving hymns. We are opening up our lives to so much more. If we are prepared for what we are facing, the less influence the enemy will have on our lives, and the more we will be witness to God's most spectacular power. Our God is a God of love, but also a God full of wrath and ferocity that is unmatched, and as the war storms all around, He is whom we want to be standing with - both now and in the end.

"I saw heaven standing open and there before me was a white horse, whose rider is called Faithful and True. With justice he judges and wages war. His eyes are like blazing fire, and on his head are many crowns. He has a name written on him that no one knows but he himself. He is dressed in a robe dipped in blood, and his name is the Word of God...He treads the winepress of the fury of the wrath of God Almighty" (Revelation 19: 11-13, 15).

We should not live a day in our lives without acknowledging the event truly taking place: this is a world most certainly at war. Though the devil is fierce, strong in all his ways, our Lord is a mighty Warrior capable of thwarting all who oppose Him. We must aim to be fit, willing and ready to stand beside Christ in battle. To be highly trained and diligent to follow. To be focused on the task at hand. To be prepared.

OohRah.

Soldiers of Christ Arise (C. Wesley)

Soldiers of Christ, arise, and put your armour on,
Strong in the strength which God supplies through His eternal Son.
Strong in the Lord of hosts, and in His mighty power,
Who in the strength of Jesus trusts is more than conqueror.

Stand then against your foes, in close and firm array;
Legions of wily fiends oppose throughout the evil day.
But meet the sons of night, and mock their vain design,
Armed in the arms of heavenly light, of righteousness divine.

Pray without ceasing, pray, your Captain gives the word;
His summons cheerfully obey and call upon the Lord;
To God your every want in instant prayer display,
Pray always; pray and never faint; pray, without ceasing, pray!

In fellowship alone, to God with faith draw near;
Approach His courts, besiege His throne with all the powers of prayer;
Go to His temple, go, nor from His altar move;
Let every house His worship know, and every heart His love.

From strength to strength go on, wrestle and fight and pray,
Tread all the powers of darkness down and win the well fought day.
Still let the Spirit cry in all His soldiers, "Come!"
Till Christ the Lord descends from high and takes the conquerors
home.

2 BATTLE TACTICS - CONTENDING FOR THE FAITH (TOM HYLAND)

"Dear friends, although I was very eager to write to you about the salvation we share, I felt I had to write and urge you to contend for the faith that was once for all entrusted to the saints" (Jude v.3).

When Jude wrote these words, he was hinting that conflict and struggle would be normal for Christians. The Christian Faith would never be popular or accepted by the world in general; people living by it would always be a despised minority. Jesus warned His apostles that they would encounter constant opposition during their lifetime, that the struggle would continue after they had gone and that it would reach its peak in the great falling away at the end of the age.

What is this "Faith" which Jude urged the saints to contend for? Faith (the Greek word is "pistis") is a common New Testament word, meaning belief or trust. In some passages it is used to describe what is believed - a collection or body of beliefs. This is the meaning of the term "the Faith" in Jude 3 and in some other places, such as:

"...a large number of priests became obedient to the faith" (Acts 6:7).

"...strengthening the disciples and encouraging them to remain true to the faith" (Acts 14:22).

"Be on your guard; stand firm in the faith; be courageous; be strong" (1 Corinthians 16:13).

In some cases, the people who hold and practise this body of beliefs are identified with them. So Paul:

"...persecuted the church of God and tried to destroy it" (Galatians 1:13),

but later preached:

"...the faith he once tried to destroy" (Galatians 1:23).

"The Faith" must be guarded at all costs

When urging the saints to contend for the Faith, Jude used the Greek word "agon" (a contest) strengthened by the prefix "epi." Translators have added the word "earnestly" in some versions to emphasise the intensity with which the saints should struggle to defend their heritage. The battle is to be fought with all the urgency of a military operation. The Faith was "entrusted" (Greek, "paradidomi", handed over) to the saints: a priceless, imperishable deposit. There is an interesting use of the word paradidomi in the phrase: "...you have come to obey from your heart the pattern of teaching that has now claimed your allegiance" (Romans 6:17).

The teaching was not only entrusted to the saints; they also were entrusted to the teaching. The picture here is of pouring metal into a mould which gives shape to what is cast in it. The saints lived the teaching in practice and conduct.

"The Faith" is the revealed will of God for His people

It was communicated on the Lord's authority by the apostles and prophets of the "new covenant". Under the "old covenant" the people of Israel were entrusted with a written record, described in Romans 3 as "the very words of God."

This record was "God-breathed" (2 Timothy 3:16) and there is no doubt that it was supported by Jesus. In the same way, God gave His "new covenant" people a written revelation with the same divine authority as the Old Testament Scriptures (see 2 Peter 3:15-16). The Faith is built into these completed Scriptures. The apostles and their co-workers placed the last stones in the building of divine revelation; that is why Jude says the Faith was once for all entrusted to the saints.

"The Faith" is comprehensive and it doesn't change

There have been no amendments or additions. Here, and only here, lies the authority for Christian teaching and practice. It is here that you will find the critical truth relating to:
  - the Person and work of our Lord Jesus
  - God's way of salvation
  - the Church which is Christ's Body
  - the second coming
  - the gathering of disciples in collective testimony in Churches of God
  - the kingdom of God
  - the house of God

In short, it is the entire teaching of the Lord in its purity - all the will of God for the people of God. What a precious heritage! Jude's appeal by the Holy Spirit is a stirring challenge to the loyal disciples of the Lord.

The battle for the Faith was valiantly fought by the apostles and their fellow-soldiers during those early pioneer years of Christian outreach. The challenge didn't only come from outside but also from enemies inside the new churches. In his short epistle Jude is concerned about this phase of the conflict. Certain men, he writes: "...have secretly slipped in among you. They are ungodly people, who pervert the grace of our God into a licence for immorality and deny Jesus Christ our only Sovereign and Lord" (Jude v.4).

He saw the danger and warned of the consequences. If these men weren't restrained they would corrupt the churches from the inside. In his address to the Ephesian elders at Miletus the apostle Paul gave a similar warning: "I know that after I leave, savage wolves will come in among you and will not spare the flock. Even from your own number men will arise and distort the truth in order to draw away disciples after them. So be on your guard!" (Acts 20:29-31).

History reveals the total accuracy of this forecast! While persecution from outside had a purifying influence and even tended to unite the saints in defence of their heritage, the infiltration of evil men and the destructive heresies of false teachers inside led to serious departure from the Faith. The relevance to today of Jude's urging to contend (earnestly) for the Faith is very clear.

Battle Quotes

"The story of your life is the story of a long and brutal assault on your heart by the one who knows what you could be and fears it." (John Eldredge)

"Theoden: I will not risk open war! Aragorn: Open war is upon you whether you risk it or not." (JRR Tolkien)

"We have all eternity to celebrate our victories, but only one short hour before sunset in which to win them." (Robert Moffat)

"When a Christian shuns fellowship with other Christians, the devil smiles. When he stops studying the Bible, the devil laughs. When he stops praying, the devil shouts for joy." (Corrie Ten Boom)

"Humanity falls into two equal and opposite errors concerning the devil – either taking the devil too seriously or not seriously enough." (C.S. Lewis)

"Temptation is no cause for dismay, but it is no excuse for sin either." (John White)

"You cannot stop birds from flying about your head – but you can prevent them from building a nest in your hair." (Martin Luther)

3 BATTLING AGAINST...DISCOURAGEMENT (GEORGE PRASHER)

"Why, my soul, are you downcast? Why so disturbed within me?" (Psalm 42:11).

The Psalms are like a mirror. We see in them, reflected from the experience of men long ago, the same thoughts which come and go in our own hearts. There are times of depression and weariness when the soul seems overclouded with gloom. They can be dangerous times. For our arch-enemy is adept at exploiting our weakness and, when discouragement darkens the spirit, he is ready to thrust home the taunting question, "Where is your God?"

The Psalmist felt this reproach like a sword in the bones. Reproach is a sword that strikes at the heart of our faith in the living God. The insinuation is that if we have a living God who loves and cares for us, why should He allow the troubles which have cast us down? In Psalms 42 and 43, each fiery dart of doubt was quenched by the large shield of faith, a faith repeated so triumphantly: "Put your hope in God, for I will yet praise Him." Yet, despite their brilliant faith, some of God's greatest servants have been discouraged in trials of a different type.

Discouraged by Disappointed Hope (1 Kings 19)

No wonder Elijah's hopes had soared! Fire from heaven had vindicated God's Name; the prophets of Baal had been vanquished; abundant rain had been poured out in response to his fervent prayer. Surely all this would lead to national repentance and revival! It seemed not, for Jezebel still despised the riches of God's goodness and his patience. Unrepentant, she would treasure up more wrath for herself in the day of judgement. Elijah fled before her murderous threat. The clouds of hopelessness and despair blanketed his spirit as he lay beneath the juniper tree. This great disappointment affected him deeply. He lamented the failure of his mission; he prayed that he might die; he said that he was the only one left in all of Israel who was loyal to God.

Discouragement had coloured his whole outlook so that he no longer saw things as God saw them. For God's purposes would march on despite the disappointing anti-climax after Carmel. Elisha would pursue his marvellous ministry in Israel; Ahab and Jezebel would be destroyed; there were still seven thousand known to God in Israel who had never compromised with Baal; Elijah himself would never die! God dealt very tenderly with his discouraged prophet.

We, too, have disappointed hopes. With us there is at times a tendency to be cast down if the type of blessing we hoped for does not follow a time of special testimony in the gospel. This aspect of things may fill our vision so that we do not see in their true perspective other important aspects of our testimony. Because a certain pattern of response by the unsaved has not followed our witness, Satan asks our discouraged souls, "Where is your God?" Elijah's God is our God. He is able to revive and strengthen us, and restore our spiritual balance, as we get alone with Him to hear again the still small voice of the Spirit.

Would Elijah's testimony at Carmel have had any greater value to God if there had followed the national revival for which the prophet craved? No, he was fulfilling his responsibility in God's service, whether they heard or not. His self-reproach and unhappiness were unwarranted. We may harm ourselves by a similar reaction to disappointing results from our testimony. For whatever the apparent results may be in a world that is getting harder and harder towards the time of the end, we have been called to a separate witness in the Churches of God. We have been called out to give effect to the whole will of God.

With all the limitations which this may impose on the scale of our gospel testimony, our calling in separated testimony to the truth is an aspect of God's purpose in our time towards which we have a special responsibility. We should pray for a right balance and refuse to allow discouragement to upset our understanding of the place God has assigned us in testimony to the truth for our time. Nor does this imply diffidence as to exercise in the gospel. Yearning for the lost, prayerful concern and zeal in gospel witness should all be ours; but these things we should do and not leave the other undone.

Discouraged Through Burdens of Responsibility

"...why have you brought this trouble on your servant? What have I done to displease you that you put the burden of all these people on me? Did I conceive all these people? Did I give them birth? Why do you tell me to carry them in my arms, as a nurse carries an infant, to the land you promised on oath to their ancestors? Where can I get meat for all these people? They keep wailing to me, 'Give us meat to eat!' I cannot carry all these people by myself; the burden is too heavy for me. If this is how you are going to treat me, please go ahead and kill me - if I have found favour in your eyes - and do not let me face my own ruin" (Numbers 11:11-15).

This does seem strange language from the lips of Moses, the man of God! Yet glancing over the period from Marah (Exodus 15:28) to Taberah (Numbers 11:8), we can appreciate a little of what this great man had borne in his leadership of God's people. He had known a tremendous strain of responsibility, which could be only partly relieved by Jethro's wise advice (Exodus 18). There had been successive crises of rebellion against God and it is a wearing thing to be faced with repeated opposition and unreasonable criticism from those to who you might rightly look for loyal support. Israel's simmering unbelief boiled up in angry rebellion whenever the heat of trial was intensified. Now the mixed multitude had fallen to the sin of lust and Israel longed for life back in Egypt.

Moses heard the people weeping throughout their families and the chilly discouragement pervading the camp entered into his own soul. With his eyes momentarily off the great Burden-Bearer, he felt distracted by the weight of responsibility he was called upon to bear and so came the outpouring of his complaint before the Lord, asking Him to relieve him of the leadership of Israel and choosing to die instead. God's purposes were very different! Years of useful service yet lay before Moses. He wouldn't die until the people reached the borders of Canaan for the second time, having first viewed the promised land.

When Moses was beside himself, God graciously made allowance for his circumstances and enabled him to regain his balance. To many who bear heavy responsibility among God's people, there may come times of similar despair. Do the problems seem too complex, the support insufficient? Does Satan challenge "Where is your God?" Then draw fresh courage from Moses' experience, when God drew him up from the slough of despond to set his feet once more upon the high places of trust and triumph.

Discouraged Through Misunderstanding God's Purpose

"When John, who was in prison, heard about the deeds of the Messiah, he sent his disciples to ask him, 'Are you the one who is to come, or should we expect someone else?' Jesus replied, 'Go back and report to John what you hear and see: The blind receive sight, the lame walk, those who have leprosy are cleansed, the deaf hear, the dead are raised, and the good news is proclaimed to the poor. Blessed is anyone who does not stumble on account of me'" (Matthew 11:2-6).

John the Baptist's question from prison was the enquiry of a man baffled and cast down by an unexpected turn of events. His discouraged soul groped for a solution of the strange problem why he should be unjustly imprisoned after the great stirring in Israel as a result of his call to repentance in preparation of the way of the Lord. Our thoughts are not God's thoughts! We may have in our own minds a pattern which we feel should develop if God is using our lives, while all the time God's plan for us may be far otherwise. John was to glorify God through death as a relatively young man. He would earn the Master's highest commendation (Matthew 11:11), yet at this point he was disturbed because he had not understood the purpose of God in his suffering.

With gracious understanding the Lord Jesus met John's enquiry. In the presence of John's messengers, many mighty works were done. They were sent to testify to John of all they had seen and heard. The Lord Jesus knows how to sustain with words him that is weary. Although He never Himself fell or was discouraged, He nevertheless appreciated the frailty of His servants. As we wait on Him, He will reassure us, perhaps by correcting our mistaken notions of the particular purpose He has in our lives.

Discouraged by Overwhelming Suffering

"Why is light given to those in misery, and life to the bitter of soul, to those who long for death that does not come, who search for it more than for hidden treasure" (Job 3:20-21).

The loss of all his children, his possessions and his health had been Job's unhappy lot - a fiery furnace of affliction, heated seven times. The most distressing feature was that he had been "blameless and upright, a man that fears God and shuns evil" (Job 1:8). In his heart rankled the question which has troubled the mind of many a sufferer since – "Why?" The adversary was not far away with his sinister challenge, "Where is your God?" for through Job's wife he urged, "Are you still maintaining your integrity? Curse God and die."

But Job did not renounce God. He kept his integrity and spoke correctly about Him. His faith and patience triumphed although the trial brought ordeals of deep discouragement, when his spirit was overwhelmed with sorrow. From Job's experience many sufferers have drawn encouragement during their times of trial. They have been helped to look beyond the things that are seen to the related unseen things. For Job in his wretchedness, keeping his integrity although baffled and dismayed, was the object of heaven's wondering delight. Satan was rebuffed in the presence of God through the sorrows of Job on earth. There may still often be that same connection between the sufferings of some of God's saints and the great unseen conflict where spiritual values are put so severely to the test and where God chooses to magnify His triumphs through the weakness of the earthen vessel.

"Be alert and of sober mind. Your enemy the devil prowls around like a roaring lion looking for someone to devour. Resist him, standing firm in the faith, because you know that the family of believers throughout the world is undergoing the same kind of sufferings. And the God of all grace, who called you to his eternal glory in Christ, after you have suffered a little while, will himself restore you and make you strong, firm and steadfast. To him be the power for ever and ever. Amen" (1 Peter 5:8-11).

The A to Z of Satan - A/B

The Bible gives Satan different names, which give a fuller picture of who he is and what he does:

- Abaddon/Angel of the Abyss/Apollyon - "They had as king over them the angel of the Abyss, whose name in Hebrew is Abaddon and in Greek is Apollyon (that is, Destroyer)" (Revelation 9:11).
- Accuser - "Then I heard a loud voice in heaven say: '...the accuser of our brothers and sisters, who accuses them before our God day and night, has been hurled down'" (Revelation 12:10).
- Adversary - "...your adversary the devil walks about like a roaring lion seeking whom he may devour..." (1 Peter 5:8 NKJV).
- Angel of light - "...Satan himself masquerades as an angel of light" (2 Corinthians 11:14).
- Anointed cherub - "You were anointed as a guardian cherub, for so I ordained you" (Ezekiel 28:14)
- Antichrist - "...every spirit that does not acknowledge Jesus is not from God. This is the spirit of the antichrist, which you have heard is coming..." (1 John 4:3)
- Beast - "...if anyone worships the beast and its image and receives its mark on their forehead or on their hand, they, too, will drink the wine of God's fury..." (Revelation 14:9-10).
- Beelzebub - "But when the Pharisees heard this, they said, 'It is only by Beelzebub, the prince of demons, that this fellow drives out demons.'" (Matthew 12:24).
- Belial - "What harmony is there between Christ and Belial? Or

what does a believer have in common with an unbeliever?" (2 Corinthians 6:15).

4 BATTLE TACTICS - SPIRITUAL WRESTLING (ALEX REID)

How do we define spiritual wrestling? What has spiritual wrestling got to do with angels? Is there a link between the two? Does our spiritual wrestling have an effect beyond our world Perhaps the most enduring biblical image of a wrestler is that of Jacob and his wrestling match at the Jabbok River. It was there that he prevailed with God and secured the blessing he was after. Although this was a physical experience, leaving its lasting mark in Jacob's body, it was also a spiritual experience, teaching Jacob reliance on God rather than his own wits. This famous wrestling match is often used as an apt illustration of persevering in prayer. The New Testament also establishes a link with spiritual struggle or wrestling and persevering in prayer:

"For our struggle (wrestling - NKJV) is not against flesh and blood, but against the rulers, against the authorities, against the powers of this dark world and against the spiritual forces of evil in the heavenly realms...pray in the Spirit on all occasions with all kinds of prayers and requests. With this in mind, be alert and always keep on praying..." (Ephesians 6:12-18).

Who are these spiritual forces of wickedness that the apostle alludes to, against whom the believer must wrestle in prayer? The experience of another Old Testament character, Daniel the prophet, helps on this question. In Daniel chapter 10 we learn something about the nature of these unseen forces. A respected Christian writer offers the following comment on Daniel chapter 10: "...creation is divided, as it appears, into a number of provinces, the material and spiritual organization of which is entrusted to a definite angel prince as, so to speak, the viceroy of God. Thus there are angels for ... whole lands and nations, as Persia (Daniel 10:13), Greece (Daniel 10:20), Israel (Daniel 10:21; 12:1). This assumes that in the world of light as also in the world of darkness there are angel organizations, which wield power in certain regions and hold ranks differing according to the size of the respective areas."

Daniel chapter 10 also implies a link between the prayers of a godly man and events in the unseen angelic sphere. The chapter sees Daniel engaged in a three week long exercise of prayer and fasting. At the end of the three weeks an angel appears to him in response to his prayer. Although we're not specifically told the subject of the prophet's prayers, the angel's message to Daniel implies that it was about God's plans for the future of the people of Israel, because the message takes in the sweep of human history from Daniel's day through to the events of the end times, especially as it affects the Israel nation.

The angel explains to Daniel that, from the first day of his prayer exercise, he, the angel, was dispatched to Daniel with a vision. The three week delay in the angel executing his mission was due to opposition from the Prince of Persia. The Prince of Persia was another angelic being who stood against the purposes of God. Since the period of delay experienced by the angelic messenger matches exactly with the length of Daniel's prayer vigil, it suggests a link between Daniel's prayer and the angel's victory over the Prince of Persia. So things prayed for on earth have an effect in the heavens.

If we're to secure the blessings we are looking for in our earthly spiritual service, we must first overcome the unseen opposition. In the example of Daniel we can see that this conflict is entered into through prayer.

Having described the parts of spiritual armour with which the believer is equipped - both defensive and offensive - Paul sounds the call to arms: "And pray in the Spirit on all occasions with all kinds of prayers and requests. With this in mind, be alert and always keep on praying for all the Lord's people" (Ephesians 6:18).

Two things sustain the spiritual warrior in this conflict: the incomparable armament with which he or she is equipped (see Ephesians 6:11-17), and the knowledge that the hostile forces are already beaten, for they were defeated by the Christ of Calvary: "And having disarmed the powers and authorities, he made a public spectacle of them, triumphing over them by the cross." (Colossians 2:15) What joy to know that we are on the winning side!

The Evolutionary Threat (Guy Jarvie)

How strong and successful the powers of darkness have been in their attacks on the minds of men! The theory of evolution has swept through the scientific and educational world discrediting the Bible in the minds of most and even of the young. This has been a powerful weapon in the adversary's hands.

The Christian must guard his mind from the imaginations and reasonings of men. The adversary has turned the minds of men from eternal things, making it much more difficult to reach men for Christ. Against this onslaught we must: "...be strong in the Lord, and in his mighty power" (Ephesians 6:10). No mere mental ability or education will equip us to stand against the power and cunning of the world-rulers of this darkness. "...If any of you think you are wise by the standards of this age, you should become "fools" so that you may become wise" (1 Corinthians 3:18). Fools for Christ's sake. As the hymn-writer said: "Our strength is in His might, His might alone."

5 THE BATTLE IN PRINT (MARTIN JONES)

Fiction writers have got their teeth into the subject of spiritual warfare for hundreds of years and it's no surprise when you think about the drama and the imagery that it throws up. Mainstream books, like Angels and Demons, might have been written for fame and fortune but Christian writers have used this opportunity to present the gospel in a very powerful and compelling way and, in a number of cases, have penetrated successfully into mainstream culture.

It is worth remembering of course, that all these books are works of fiction and contain imaginative story elements that draw from outside the Bible itself – so they shouldn't be used as a replacement for your own Bible study! But, that said, here is a quick run-down of some of the most famous of them that you might want to take a look at:

The Holy War – John Bunyan (1682)

The Holy War is quite possibly the grand-father of them all. John Bunyan's most famous book is Pilgrim's Progress (see below), but he wrote over fifty others. One of them is The Holy War, an allegorical novel which depicts fictional people and events to illustrate the Christian's spiritual journey.

The Holy War is the story of "Mansoul", a perfect town built for the glory of its benevolent creator and leader, King Shaddai. After being deceived by the wicked ruler Diabolus, the town rejects the rule of King Shaddai and falls deep into the mires of sin and despair. As battles rage between good and evil, the redemption of Mansoul is only possible through the victory of Shaddai's son, Prince Emmanuel.

Bunyan's allegory is full of clever characters and captivating drama. This important Christian classic is both educational and entertaining, so it is a great book for leisure reading or a link into a Bible study. Overall, this book has stood the test of time pretty well. You have to bear in mind that the book was written over 300 years ago and so the language can be pretty old-fashioned at times; but if you persevere you will get used to it eventually!

The Pilgrim's Progress (from This World to That Which Is to Come) – John Bunyan (1678)

This book is regarded as one of the most significant works of religious English literature and it has been translated into more than 200 languages. It has never been out of print. The (relatively) easy style of the book has meant that readers of all ages can understand the spiritual significance of the depictions in the story, and quite a number of versions have been specially produced for children.

In a sense, Bunyan was undergoing his own personal battle when he wrote the book. When he began it, he was in jail for violations of the Conventicle Act, which prohibited the holding of religious services outside the authority of the established Church of England. Part One of the story tells of "Christian" and his journey to the "Celestial City" (heaven) where he meets a colourful cast of characters and lots of trials and tribulations along the way. The critical part of the story comes where Christian comes to the cross and the great burden he is carrying on his back (sin) falls away. Part Two tells of the subsequent journey of Christian's wife Christiana and their children to the Celestial City.

Did you know?

- Famous Christian preacher C.H Spurgeon was influenced by The Pilgrim's Progress and is said to have read the book over 100 times.
- Pilgrim's Progress is listed as one of Mr Tulliver's books in George Eliot's The Mill on the Floss.
- Samuel Johnson, the father of the modern dictionary, said that "this is the great merit of the book, that the most cultivated man cannot find anything to praise more highly, and the child knows nothing more amusing."

The Lion, the Witch and the Wardrobe – C.S. Lewis (1950)

The Lion, the Witch and the Wardrobe is a fantasy novel for children by C.S. Lewis. The story revolves around four young children - Lucy, Peter, Edmund and Susan - who disappear into a strange land called Narnia via the back of an old wardrobe. They soon find themselves in a battle over Narnia between good and evil, the latter characterised by the White Witch (who has put Narnia into permanent winter) and Aslan, the great Lion, who is put to death by the Witch's followers. His death not only frees Edmund from the penalty of a recent treacherous act, but also frees Narnia from its long winter. The presentation of the gospel is completely clear and is very movingly presented.

The book was published in 1950. It is the first-published book of The Chronicles of Narnia and the best known book of the series. Although it was written and published first, it is second in the series' internal chronological order, after The Magician's Nephew. Time magazine included the novel in its "TIME 100 Best English-language Novels from 1923 to 2005." It has also been published in 47 foreign languages.

C.S. Lewis (1898-1963) was a novelist, poet, academic, medievalist, literary critic, essayist, lay theologian and Christian apologist from Belfast, Ireland. He is known for both his fictional work, especially The Screwtape Letters, The Chronicles of Narnia and The Space Trilogy and his nonfiction, such as Mere Christianity, Miracles and The Problem of Pain. A close friend of the author, J.R.R. Tolkien, Lewis is widely regarded as one of the finest minds of modern times and one of the most respected Christian theologians.

Did you know?

- The Chronicles of Narnia: The Lion, the Witch and the Wardrobe film was released in 2005 by Walt Disney Pictures, with the voice of Aslan played by Liam Neeson.
- The DVD version was the best seller of 2006.

The Last Battle – C.S. Lewis (1956)

The Last Battle is the seventh and final book in The Chronicles of Narnia. The preceding books in the series all contain various phases of the conflict between good and evil and all are highly recommended reading for all ages. (A recent book The Narnia Code goes into tremendous detail regarding the masses of hidden meanings and allegory that C.S. Lewis included that would be totally missed by the young reader, but appreciated by the careful, older student.)

The Last Battle is where the conflict becomes most visible and final. The citizens of Narnia are tricked by an imposter Aslan and many join his side against the real Aslan. When the real Aslan finally triumphs in the Battle, the Narnians are held to account and judged according to their response to Aslan - those loyal to him are taken on to "Aslan's Country" and the opponents are taken to an unmentioned place. Narnia is then obliterated in a series of events.

The Left Behind Series – Jerry B. Jenkins and Tim LaHaye (1995-2007)

The sixteen books of the Left Behind series have what has been called a "Christian, dispensationalist, pre-millenialist eschatological viewpoint of the end of the world." In other words, they hold to the traditional, evangelical view that:

- The book of Revelation (and parts of Daniel, Isaiah and Ezekiel) is prophetic and speaks to a future time where the events described there will actually happen.
- All believers will be "raptured" by the coming of Jesus to the air.
- There will then come an Antichrist who sets himself up as God and will force people to take the mark of the beast or face execution during the "Great Tribulation."
- There is such a thing as a literal millennium, which will be a thousand years reign on earth by Jesus, post-tribulation and prior to the Last Judgement.

When true believers in Christ have been "raptured", it leaves the world shattered and chaotic. As people scramble for answers, a relatively unknown Romanian politician named Nicolae Carpathia rises to become secretary-general of the United Nations, promising to restore peace and stability to all nations. What most of the world does not realize is that Carpathia is actually the Antichrist foretold from the Bible. Coming to grips with the truth and becoming born-again Christians, Rayford Steele, his daughter Chloe, their pastor Bruce Barnes, and young journalist Cameron "Buck" Williams begin their quest as the Tribulation Force to help save the lost and prepare for the coming Tribulation, in which God will rain down judgement on the world for seven years.

The series has been adapted into three action thriller films: "Left Behind: The Movie", "Left Behind II: Tribulation Force" and "Left Behind: World at War." The series also inspired the PC game "Left Behind: Eternal Forces" and its sequels, "Left Behind: Tribulation Forces" and "Left Behind 3: Rise of the Antichrist." The subject matter and the often graphic descriptions mean that the series is not suitable for under-12's.

Did you know?

- In 1998, the first four books of the series held the top four slots in the New York Times' best-seller list simultaneously, despite the fact that the New York Times' best-seller list does not take Protestant bookstore sales into account. Book 10 debuted at number one on this list.
- Total sales for the series have surpassed 65 million copies.
- One reason often cited for the books' popularity is the quick pacing and action. Michelle Goldberg has written that, "On one level, the attraction of the Left Behind books isn't that much different from that of, say, Tom Clancy or Stephen King. The plotting is brisk and the characterizations Manichean. People disappear and things blow up."

The Screwtape Letters – C.S. Lewis (1942)

The Screwtape Letters is a satirical Christian apologetic novel written in a letter style. The letters provide a series of lessons in the importance of taking a deliberate role in living out Christian faith by portraying a typical human life (and areas as diverse as sex, love, pride, gluttony and war), with all its temptations and failings, as seen from the viewpoints of the devils.

A senior demon, Screwtape, holds an administrative post in the bureaucracy ("Lowerarchy") of Hell and acts as a mentor to his nephew, Wormwood, the inexperienced tempter. Wormwood needs advice on how to secure the damnation of a British man, known only as "the Patient."

In the thirty-one letters which make up the book, Screwtape gives Wormwood detailed advice on various methods of undermining faith and promoting sin in the Patient, interspersed with observations on human nature and Christian doctrine. Wormwood and Screwtape live in a peculiarly morally reversed world, where individual benefit and greed are seen as the greatest good, and neither demon is capable of comprehending or acknowledging true human virtue when he sees it.

In Letter 22, after several weeks of attempts to find a loose woman for the Patient, and when Screwtape receives a painful punishment for a secret he divulges to Wormwood about God's genuine love for humanity, the irate Screwtape notes that the Patient has fallen in love with a Christian girl and he is enraged over this mistake that Wormwood has allowed. Toward the end of this letter, Screwtape becomes so incensed that he turns into a large centipede, mimicking a similar transformation that John Milton included in Book 10 of Paradise Lost, where the demons were raging so much against God that they found they had been turned into snakes.

In the last letter, it emerges that the Patient has been killed during an air raid (World War II having broken out between the fourth and fifth letters), and has gone to Heaven. Wormwood is to be punished for letting a soul "slip through his fingers" by being handed over to the fate that would have awaited his Patient had he been successful: the consumption of his spiritual essence by the other demons.

Did you know?

- Ex-US Vice-Presidential candidate Sarah Palin has written that the book "touched me with clarity as it pertained to faith and purpose."
- Both The Screwtape Letters and the sequel Screwtape Proposes a Toast have been released on both audio cassette and CD, with narration by John Cleese and Joss Ackland. A dramatized audio version by Focus on the Family was a 2010 Audie Award finalist.
- In the 1995 music video "Hold Me, Thrill Me, Kiss Me, Kill Me" by U2, an animated Bono is seen walking down the street holding the book The Screwtape Letters.
- The Screwtape Letters is one of Lewis' most popular works, although he claimed that it was "not fun" to write, and "resolved never to write another 'Letter'."

This Present Darkness – Frank Peretti (1986)

This Present Darkness was Peretti's first published novel for adults and shows contemporary views on angels, demons, prayer and spiritual warfare as demons and angels interact and struggle for control of the citizens of the small town of Ashton. It is critical of Eastern and New Age spiritual practices, portraying meditation as a means of demonic possession.

The book has achieved remarkable sales success, selling in excess of 2.5 million copies worldwide and remaining on the Christian top ten best-sellers list for over 150 consecutive weeks after its release. Its title comes from Ephesians 6:12 (ESV): "For we do not wrestle against flesh and blood, but against the rulers, against the authorities, against the cosmic powers over this present darkness, against the spiritual forces of evil in the heavenly places."

Did you know?

- A track called Ashton (the name of the town in the novel) on the

Michael W. Smith album i2 (EYE) is inspired by the book.
· Peretti followed This Present Darkness with a sequel in 1988 called Piercing the Darkness.

Am I a Soldier of the Cross?

Am I a soldier of the cross,
A follower of the Lamb,
And shall I fear to own His cause,
Or blush to speak His Name?

Must I be carried to the skies
On flowery beds of ease,
While others fought to win the prize,
And sailed through bloody seas?

Are there no foes for me to face?
Must I not stem the flood?
Is this vile world a friend to grace,
To help me on to God?

Sure I must fight if I would reign;
Increase my courage, Lord.
I'll bear the toil, endure the pain,
Supported by Thy Word.

Thy saints in all this glorious war,
Shall conquer, though they die;
They see the triumph from afar,
By faith's discerning eye.

When that illustrious day shall rise,
And all Thy armies shine,
In robes of victory through the skies,
The glory shall be Thine.
(Isaac Watts)

6 DESPATCHES FROM THE FRONT LINE – THE MISSIONARY (MARK IMOUKHUEDE)

Q: Mark, tell us a little bit about how you started life....

A: I was born into a polygamous non-Christian family – one father, three wives and 18 children. We lived in a three bedroom flat; my father had one room to himself, my mum and her children had one of the two rooms remaining and the number three wife lived with her parents in another part of the city. My father was a native doctor and an idolater. His room was his office where he carried out his trade and I grew up helping him to carry out the chores relating to it.

Q: How did you ever come to hear the gospel in that environment?

A: Thankfully, my father knew the value of education although he did not go beyond primary school level himself. He therefore didn't oppose anything we did that could give us more education than he had – so we went to any church within the community to learn. I was about 12 years old when I gave serious thoughts to what I had been hearing in Sunday School. John 3:16, and the love of God through His Son, was well taught and I received Jesus Christ as my personal Saviour by faith. Three of my sisters had been baptised after the assurance of their salvation the year before and had been added to the Church of God in Surulere, Lagos, Nigeria. I followed in their steps and was baptised too and added to the church. This was my early beginning as a Christian.

Q: How did you decide to become a missionary?

A: The call of God to full time work as a missionary was very clear although it took me three years to say "Yes" to the Lord. It all started in 1983 at a funeral service of one of our African missionaries in his village of Akarakumoh, Lagos State, Nigeria. The Bible passage read was Joshua 1:1-2. The service went on but I seemed not to be there in the hall. I was in tears pleading to the Lord that it could not be me. On returning home after the funeral, I went back to the Bible passage in Joshua and read up to verse 9. The promises that God gave Joshua were to be mine:

"After the death of Moses the servant of the Lord, the Lord said to Joshua son of Nun, Moses' aide: 'Moses my servant is dead. Now then, you and all these people, get ready to cross the Jordan River into the land I am about to give to them - to the Israelites. I will give you every place where you set your foot, as I promised Moses. Your territory will extend from the desert to Lebanon, and from the great river, the Euphrates - all the Hittite country - to the Mediterranean Sea in the west. No one will be able to stand against you all the days of your life. As I was with Moses, so I will be with you; I will never leave you nor forsake you. Be strong and courageous, because you will lead these people to inherit the land I swore to their ancestors to give them.

Be strong and very courageous. Be careful to obey all the law my servant Moses gave you; do not turn from it to the right or to the left, that you may be successful wherever you go. Keep this Book of the Law always on your lips; meditate on it day and night, so that you may be careful to do everything written in it. Then you will be prosperous and successful. Have I not commanded you? Be strong and courageous. Do not be afraid; do not be discouraged, for the LORD your God will be with you wherever you go.'" (Joshua 1:1-9)

Three years followed, still seeking the assurance of the Lord that this was not some wishful thinking of mine. My wife was very supportive and gave the encouragement to go forward - despite going from known to unknown as far as our future family upkeep would be concerned. I was a school teacher in a high school. I had worked for nine years and would be leaving the service without any entitlements. But God had called and all His promises will not fail. Twenty five years ago, I was commended to full time missionary service by the Fellowship of the Churches of God spread all over the world. Twenty five years on and He has remained faithful. Praise God!

Q: Tell us about your some of the early missionary work and the challenges that you faced...

A: My first work outside Nigeria was in 1989 to pioneer the establishment of the Church of God in Ghana. It was not easy for my wife and two children, as well as myself of course. I will always thank God for my family who have invested so much in my life. I cannot thank them enough for their understanding and support in every way. Travelling by road to Ghana takes about 12-13 hours as one has to go through two countries, Benin and Togo, with six borders with immigration and custom check points - in addition to the challenges of the bad conditions of the roads.

It so happens that when these security officers at the borders see the foreign number plates of your vehicle, they then try to be a little difficult. The Lord always kept His word to see me through. Now we have two assemblies in Ghana. The first was planted in 1994 and the second in 2012. One may wonder why it took so long! There were initial challenges of acceptance of the "foreigner" into the community, funding for the work was another challenge and other churches were afraid that they may lose their members to this foreigner – sometimes it was even a bit on the unfriendly side. It takes time to prove oneself as sent from God. But twenty three years after, one can look back with thankfulness to God that the work in Ghana can continue whether the missionary is there or not. The seed was sown, it brought forth fruit and they are continuing – praise God! That is the joy of missionary work.

Q: Is the work always joyful?

A: No, it isn't! Work in some other countries has not been as smooth sailing and it has had to be discontinued; this was my experience in Kenya and Uganda though I still have good Christian friends there until today. In 1995 I went to Kenya and Malawi with another overseer of the Churches of God in response to a "Macedonian" call to come and teach Bible truths, and the same happened in Uganda in 2000. We laboured among them as we tried to discern their seriousness. We found out that poverty, ignorance and disease go together in a vicious cycle. These confronted us very much in these countries. To be frank, some of the contacts were not honest in their dealings with us and we had to move away from such people who later made themselves as our obstacle to progress. They went to any extent to disrupt the work each time they were found out. When an unsaved man is poor, he will go to any extent to make a living instead of looking to God for his all-round survival.

Q: Many people assume that poverty makes it easier for people to accept the gospel, but that isn't necessarily the case?

A: Not necessarily. Actually, one of the biggest challenges for the missionary in Africa is to maintain the balance between the needs of the body and the soul. Take Malawi, for example – it is one of the poorest countries in the world. It ranked one of the 5 poorest in Africa and number 10 overall of the 20 poorest of the world. Extreme poverty, the rampant spread of HIV/AIDS and the widespread corruption are the banes of Malawi. The country is one of the world's least developed nations and also one of the most densely populated. But when people are gainfully employed and have some measure of education, ignorance and disease are reduced to the barest minimum and they are often more open to hear the gospel as their other needs are met. The Churches of God, through its relief programmes, have been able to set up mobile medical clinics which are attended by thousands – all of them are happy to listen to the gospel message being preached to them while they wait for medical attention.

I recall an experience while travelling to Ghana from Nigeria some years ago. The Immigration officer at one of the border points had collected my passport for the usual clearance. He then enquired, "What do you have for the flesh?" I thought that was very smart of him, so I gave him some money for a loaf of bread. As a missionary in Africa, though the primary focus is to preach the Gospel for the salvation of souls, the physical needs of the people are not overlooked:

"What good is it, my brothers and sisters, if someone claims to have faith but has no deeds? Can such faith save them? Suppose a brother or a sister is without clothes and daily food. If one of you says to them, 'Go in peace; keep warm and well fed', but does nothing about their physical needs, what good is it? In the same way, faith by itself, if it is not accompanied by action, is dead." (James 2:14-17)

I thank God because, in God's goodness, my background has enabled me to respond to matters concerning the body, soul and the spirit – particularly in countries where poverty, ignorance and disease have caused much damage and dehumanized the people.

Q: You've been a missionary for a long time now! What keeps you going?

A: Galatians 6:9, which says: "Let us not become weary in doing good, for at the proper time we will reap a harvest if we do not give up", is always a great challenge and encouragement that the labours in these far away places without family members will bear fruit someday. I recall a time in 2000 when I had to travel to Malawi – my wife was in hospital and we were expecting our third child. I was at the point of not making that trip but my wife encouraged me to go. I went to the hospital the day of my travel, spent time in prayer with her and then went to the Airport. God blessed that "doing good" at the proper time – there have been five assemblies in Malawi since 2003 and there are prospects of more, as well as fifteen or so other churches in Africa.

Q: In what ways have you felt you are in a battle?

A: The challenges have been enormous even to the point of death. There have been physical, psychological and spiritual attacks during these almost 25 years out in the work:

Physical

The word of God has revealed in John 10:10 that "the thief (the devil) comes only to steal and kill and destroy." In December 2006, after a very lovely time with the Church in Kasoa, Ghana, I was kidnapped (possibly after being drugged) on public transport on my way home. Many people have disappeared or been killed in that kind of situation in Nigeria. Who was behind it? The devil, of course! I found myself lying face down by a very busy road side the next day after being dumped there overnight. I could have been run over by a vehicle. My life has been preserved against the opposition of the devil.

Psychological

Intimidation in different ways with a view to making one afraid to carry out the mandate is a game of the devil. It takes a fearful dimension when you are not a citizen of the country where one is working. It can be so fierce that one begins to think of self rather than the ability of the Lord to overcome all the oppositions of the devil. While working in Uganda we were brought before the Police Authority with all manner of accusations by one of the leaders of the group we were visiting. We found out he was working for some American missions that had promised them so much. We decided to part ways with him because we were already making inroads, reaching the community with the Gospel without their assistance. He did not like this and so lent himself to be used by the devil. We were given 24 hours to get out of the country as our safety could no longer be guaranteed.

Spiritual

Being an arrow-head in a pioneering work is loaded with many dangers that the devil tries to exploit. Any work being carried out by a missionary is truly not "his" work. It is the Lord's work and a work he has been privileged to oversee on behalf of the community. All must give full support and be in unity in the work and with the worker, here the Missionary. Sometimes I am very conscious of the absence of this unity and support. The rest in the walk begins to diminish and the door opens for the attack of the devil. Our God is the God of peace - not the god of confusion. The devil is. Love and support from the community protects the leader and covers his faults and weaknesses as they stand in the gap for him. I have seen the spirit of dissatisfaction and strife setting in as the "accuser of the brethren" begins to work on my thought life and unity begins to fall apart; at that point it is the battle for the mind. Thank God for His Spirit and His word. God gives the victory and the peace needed in the work.

Q: With all that in mind, do you ever regret becoming a missionary?

A: Did I make a mistake to answer the call? No, never! Lives have been transformed for the better; those who, up to then, didn't know what their eternal destiny would be after death are rejoicing in the peace that God has given them in Christ Jesus. There are now around twenty Churches of God in Africa – in Nigeria, Ghana and Malawi, and soon in Liberia, God willing. For me, life as a missionary in Africa has been a great privilege. When you spend and are spent, you feel fulfilled and refreshed. I cannot know a better life.

Battle Quotes 1

"Spiritual darkness comes on horseback, and goes away on foot. It is upon us before we know that it is coming. It leaves us slowly, gradually, and not till after many days." (J.C. Ryle)

"God had one Son without sin; but He has no son without temptation." (Charles Spurgeon)

"There is a war going on. All talk of a Christian's right to live luxuriously 'as a child of the King' in this atmosphere sounds hollow - especially since the King himself is stripped for battle." (John Piper)

"If we fight the Lord's battles merely by duplicating the way the world does its work, we are like little boys playing with wooden swords pretending they are in the battle while their big brothers are away in some distant bloody land." (Francis Schaeffer)

7 BATTLE TACTICS – PERSEVERING IN PRAYER (JOHN MILLER)

Didn't the Lord tell His disciples to "watch and pray"? Doesn't it often happen that we do the praying and think that God can do the watching? Aren't we like the disciples who may have prayed when the Lord told them to pray, but they fell asleep? Paul's words to the Christian soldier are relevant when he urges the soldier in this spiritual warfare to take up the whole armour of God: "And pray in the Spirit on all occasions with all kinds of prayers and requests. With this in mind, be alert and always keep on praying for all the Lord's people" (Ephesians 6:18).

The Greek word Proskopto used in this verse, and translated here as "keep on praying", means "to strike against." It's illustrated by the words of the Lord who instructed His disciples in prayer to knock and it would be opened to them. They were to knock and to keep knocking; to ask and keep asking. We must ask like David did, for when he asked he set a watch to see when and how the Lord would answer him: "I have posted watchmen on your walls, Jerusalem; they will never be silent day or night. You who call on the LORD, give yourselves no rest..." (Isaiah 62:6).

Sometimes you hear very well thought out, well-spoken prayers which are really tributes to some of the ways or doings of God. One is almost tempted to say to the brother, "Ask something!" God is interested about doing things and we should ask Him to do them. How many things we would like Him to do, both for ourselves individually and for God's people? And, if we ask Him, do we seek after what we ask, do we persevere? We may get tired and perhaps fall asleep – and instead of praying it is snoring. Isn't it time to wake up?

We needn't go to sleep though times are bad and there is a prevailing deadness and indifference. Even though we walk through a cemetery we needn't fall asleep in it. God is alive; He is awake. He is doing His work unseen by most and He will work for us if we ask Him and seek after what we ask. He knows whether we mean it. Remember, He works for them that wait for Him: "...Though it linger, wait for it; it will certainly come and will not delay" (Habakkuk 2:3).

What seems like God's delays are not denials. If we were in His position and had His wisdom we would do exactly as He does. The Fellowship is in need of godly, praying men and women. We may not be able to preach with eloquence, but we can pray with power. We can be persistent. We can sit on God's doorstep and knock again and again. We can hold on and not let God go unless He blesses us. We can pray always and without ceasing. We may be frequent visitors to heaven. The way is there, it is free and there is the absolute freedom to speak to God through Christ. Pray as you walk, pray as you sit, pray as you lie down, pray as you stand, pray on your knees, pray always and in every place!

Ephesians 6:10-18

"Finally, be strong in the Lord and in his mighty power. Put on the full armour of God, so that you can take your stand against the devil's schemes. For our struggle is not against flesh and blood, but against the rulers, against the authorities, against the powers of this dark world and against the spiritual forces of evil in the heavenly realms. Therefore put on the full armour of God, so that when the day of evil comes, you may be able to stand your ground, and after you have done everything, to stand.

Stand firm then, with the belt of truth buckled around your waist, with the breastplate of righteousness in place, and with your feet fitted with the readiness that comes from the gospel of peace. In addition to all this, take up the shield of faith, with which you can extinguish all the flaming arrows of the evil one. Take the helmet of salvation and the sword of the Spirit, which is the word of God. And pray in the Spirit on all occasions with all kinds of prayers and requests. With this in mind, be alert and always keep on praying for all the Lord's people."

8 SHOCK AND AWE (JON NEELY)

Warning. The following program contains scenes of extreme violence, explicit content and mature subject matter. Viewer discretion is advised.

How often we see a warning such as this before a show or film. Meant to make clear to us what it is we are about to watch, and give a heads-up that the next three hours will not be of grandma reading a story by the fireplace, gently sipping a cup of Darjeeling. It is to warn us that what lies ahead is meant to be disturbing and at times shock us.

No more visible are these warnings than in features about war, which are usually filled with as much blood, guts and severed limbs as possible. We are so numb to these warnings that appear before movies that they generally serve as a few extra seconds we have to pop the remaining kernels and find our perfectly-fitted groove in the couch. We do not give them a second thought. In today's society, they are rendered meaningless.

But what if those warnings were on more than just our television screens? What if we were given warnings far more crucial to our lives than a pre-film predict? What if, immediately following our salvation, an urgent bulletin flashed overhead that informed us that our lives would be filled with explicit content, mature subject matter and that we had better prepare ourselves accordingly?

The thing is, such a warning does exist; in the form of a leather-bound guide lying beside our beds, consisting of 66 books meant to alert us that the day at hand is likely to be much more real and dangerous than we think. So we had better put the popcorn down and pay attention. Paul writes to Timothy from prison, imploring him to "...mark this: there will be terrible times in the last days" (2 Timothy 3:1). Paul did not just leave it at that; he went on to warn that: "...everyone who wants to live a godly life in Christ Jesus will be persecuted, while evildoers and impostors will go from bad to worse, deceiving and being deceived" (2 Timothy 3:12-13).

Sleep well, Timothy. Paul knew then what we so often fail to recognize now and he certainly did not beat around the bush. We have been warned. We are in these terrible end times that Paul speaks of, and they only get worse from here. We have been dropped into the middle of the battlefield, and if we plan on surviving we would be wise to pick up a sword and join the fight.

"The thief comes only to steal and kill and destroy; I have come that they may have life, and have it to the full" (John 10:10).

Satan is looking to destroy us; Christ is fighting against him so that we may live like life is meant to be lived. It is all happening right in front of us, and unlike during a movie, if what we see scares us, it will do us no good to just close our eyes. If Christ is fighting for our lives, we cannot stand by the side and hope for the best.

One reason Christians may have a problem believing we are currently engulfed in war is that we so often focus solely on Christ as the loving, kind, nurturing Man, who came to this world to heal the sick and rescue the poor - He of course is all of these things and more - but we fail to see the other side of Christ: the invincible gladiator entrenched in a long battle. Yes, the little babe who lay in a manger and grew up to go on and spread love and compassion throughout the world like no other in history just also happens to be the most ruthless, fierce, battle-tested warrior on the front lines of the most paramount war ever to be fought. Not the Sunday school image of Christ we often get, is it? We are to be loving, kind, and nurturing to others as well, of course, but that is not where it ends.

"...The reason the Son of God appeared was to destroy the devil's work" (1 John 3:8).

He was sent to save, yes, but we cannot forget what Christ was sent to save us from. There is an exceedingly wicked force working against us, and Christ intends to destroy it entirely, leaving behind not a memory. There is an immense power leading this purpose and Christ will not cease until the devil is destroyed. In 1996, the US Military composed doctrine that they referred to as Shock and Awe (or Rapid Dominance). It was meant to display powerful and overwhelming strength while destroying the very will of the adversary, leaving them paralyzed and unable to respond. They had power and they were not afraid to use it. They believed this was a tried-and-true, American-made doctrine, but of course they were not the first to employ this strategy. Shock and Awe was not only thought of long ago, but has been on display since Lucifer was thrown from the Lord's presence. God's version of Shock and Awe makes military strength look like an episode of Veggie Tales.

If it is shock and awe we want, we need look no further than the war against evil, and the power that Christ is wielding at His fingertips. Our Lord created the stars with the same ease that we add sprinkles to a cupcake - His power is unfathomable to the human mind and very much in play as we speak. We look to the news for our daily intake of shocking, awe-inspiring military power, but it is a blip on the radar compared with the monumental force of Christ. All this from the man with the gentle face and worn-out sandals we learn of from childhood, you say? We must have missed that Sunday school class. He is not interested in speaking calmly to His adversary, sitting Satan down and attempting to figure things out to the soft tune of a harp; not a chance! Christ came to Calvary to annihilate all trace of evil and it took an incredible power to do so; a power that we simply cannot fathom.

"...Resist the devil, and he will flee from you" (James 4:7).

We cite this verse with ease and with a smile on our face, but what is it exactly that we think God is saying here? Is this the same as our kindergarten teacher reminding us to "Say No To Drugs?" Fat chance, kid. The devil is not fleeing from anyone who politely asks him to go away so they can get back to their finger-paints. In order to make him flee, we must show that we mean business, that backing down is not an option. If it is a fight he wants, it is a fight he is going to get. Does the school bully, when looking to steal lunch money, tearfully retreat after being called a big meanie and asked to leave? Doubtful, and employing that plan will likely cause significant financial difficulty in your early days. Conversely, Christ put a fist through the devil's front teeth at Calvary and now has him thinking twice before walking down the same hallway. We want to be on the side of the one who has the enemy running for cover come the end. The time for talk is done. If we are standing with Him, we might want to be prepared to throw a punch or two - Christ certainly is.

Think of young David, when faced with evil in the form of a giant (not to mention an entire army standing with him). He was a mere boy, yet not once did he consider the best way to defeat his formidable foe would be by lobbing happy thoughts in the giant's general direction. David went straight out to his opponent with the confidence of a veteran in combat: "As the Philistine moved closer to attack him, David ran quickly toward the battle line to meet him" (1 Samuel 17:48).

This kid, no taller than the enemy's waist, ran towards the giant - headlong into battle - without a second thought. Then, with the power of his Heavenly Father, the boy who was tending to his sheep that morning, skillfully propelled a pebble between the giant's eyes, stood over him with a monstrous sword and brutally sliced his head off. Children today need safety scissors to wage war on paper. David trusted in the Lord's power and, because of that, the giant was slain, the bully was felled and the enemy was conquered. Shock and Awe in full affect. As for the opposing army that remained, what was their reaction when they saw the boy standing victorious? They fled. Resist the devil and he will flee. We resist by holding up our hand. David resisted by holding up the enemy's head. His definition seems more effective.

These days, some Christians scoff at examples such as this. "Times have changed," they say. "Our job now is only to spread the word of God and serve as good examples to the world." And we wonder why evil is so prevalent today. The only thing that has changed is us. God is the same as He was then, as is Satan. As for us? Well, our version of being in the army of the Lord today is watching inspirational PowerPoint presentations and holding frequent potluck dinners. Fighting evil with handshakes and Hello Dolly's. David would be so proud.

When two of the disciples, James and John, learned of a village rejecting Jesus, they responded first with, "...Lord, do you want us to call fire down from heaven to destroy them?" (Luke 9:54). That was option number one for them. That was their mindset when it came to those who opposed their Lord. Not to avoid confrontation by singing pleasant hymns in protest. No, Jesus' own disciples asked if they could call upon a raging inferno from above to obliterate those who stood against Him. It is no wonder that Christ gave them the name "Sons of Thunder" (Mark 3:17). They were off-base at the time and they were told that; but they instinctively wanted to fight evil with the radiant valour of God shining through them and boy, was it evident. These two men wanted to show no mercy – when we look at this verse, dare we say they learned that from their Lord?

"And then the lawless one will be revealed, whom the Lord Jesus will overthrow with the breath of his mouth and destroy by the splendour of his coming" (2 Thessalonians 2:8).

The time has come for us to uncover our eyes and join the fight. It is time to acknowledge that this is a God who tells us: "The righteous will be glad when they are avenged, when they dip their feet in the blood of the wicked." (Psalm 58:10) Exactly how many songs do we belt out that line for the chorus? Goodness gracious, viewer discretion indeed. This is not to say we should ease up on recognizing Christ as the Prince of Peace and the Lamb of God. By His grace we are saved, after all. But when the devil stands in our path, we only need to know who is on our side, and what He will do to the enemy: "The God of peace will soon crush Satan under your feet..." (Romans 16:20).

We cannot bask in the warm light of God's glory and then turn around in ignorance when we hear the Lord is going to stomp on the head of our adversary. Not the right to remain silent, but the authority to fight back. One must question if we truly understand what our roles are if we naturally pick and choose from the Bible what best suits our view of a "Good Christian". Besides, we would hate to get our church clothes dirty.

Want to resist the devil the way a Good Christian of today would? Best of luck, but he is not one to heed to that tune, sorry. He will continue to attack until we either succumb to his evil ways, or wake up and grasp the reality that this is a battle and that the Almighty allows us to flex our God-given, God-powered muscles. Or, as David would say:

"Break the teeth in their mouths, O God; Lord, tear out the fangs of those lions! Let them vanish like water that flows away; when they draw the bow, let their arrows fall short. May they be like a slug that melts away as it moves along, like a stillborn child that never sees the sun" (Psalm 58:6-8).

He knew the seriousness of what we are up against, and he knew the strength of our Lord. Want to resist the devil as God would see us do, as a modern-day David? Stand with the Lord in battle and be a part of the victory when Christ launches a rock between Satan's eyes and brings a heavenly fire upon his head. The overwhelming power of God can and will destroy the adversary, leaving him paralyzed. Shock and Awe; strategy of the Lord; strategy of those fighting with Him.

Warning. The following of Jesus Christ contains scenes of extreme violence, explicit content, and mature subject matter. Resisting the devil is advised.

Battling by Building

"...building yourselves up in your most holy faith and praying in the Holy Spirit..." (Jude v.20). This word "building" is an architectural term that means to renovate. It implies tearing down what's not working for you and building up what will. When you don't understand that, you are left to believe that whatever life has handed you is just the way it is and you have to take it. You'd be surprised at the number of people who go to church every week just to get a word to help them survive. They sing about faith and talk about it. But when you ask them, "How are you doing?" they say, "I'm just hangin' on. I'm just hopin' I can make it through."

Yes, there are times when that will truly be the case. But that should be the exception, not the rule. The Bible says, "We are more than conquerors..." (Romans 8:37). To be a conqueror means to fight a battle and win it. But to be more than a conqueror means to win a battle without even having to fight it. Jesus has already fought and won the battle for you. And today He is saying as He did in Luke 10:19: "I have given you authority...to overcome all the power of the enemy; nothing will harm you." You say, "How do I get this power?" Jude says we can access this power for living by praying in the Holy Spirit; and you can do it anywhere: in your car on the way to work, on your treadmill or even in your bathroom. You just need a place where you can be alone with God, praying and reading His Word, building up your faith. (UCB Word for the Day)

9 BATTLE ROUND 1 – GOD V SATAN (KEITH DORRICOTT)

Every disciple of the Lord Jesus is affected by Satan who, although a spiritual being and invisible to us, is nevertheless a very real person and a very real adversary. But, although the Bible refers to him and his actions repeatedly, we won't find a complete explanation of his beginning. Satan, in the form of a serpent, first comes to our attention in Genesis chapter 3 where we read of the fall of man. He tempted the new creature to sin in the same way as he himself had done and so cause the sin which was in him to enter the human creation. It seems clear therefore that a great deal had happened in Satan's history before the events in Eden, but we are told very little of this - obviously for our own good: "The secret things belong to the LORD our God, but the things revealed belong to us…" (Deuteronomy 29:29).

What has been revealed is that:

- Satan was created in the original creation of the angels, which preceded the creation of man;
- his was the first evil aspiration; and
- this had enormous consequences for the entire creation.

Let us look at what the Bible reveals about each:

Satan's Origin

Satan is not a divine being. He is an angel - a spirit being created by God. The creation of angels came before the work of creation that is described in detail in Genesis chapters 1 and 2; but by how long, we don't know. But Job 38:6-7 tells us that the angels (who are described as sons of God) witnessed the laying of the foundations of the earth. And yet they, too, were created because, as Colossians 1 tells us, all things in the heavens and upon the earth, visible and invisible, were created by God.

The angelic creation is vast. Although it consists of innumerable armies, they are still ordered by God. Ephesians 6:12 tells us that there are angelic principalities and powers. They are organized into legions, as human armies are (Matthew 26:53). Some have particular responsibilities on this earth - for example: for children (Matthew 18:10) and for the nation of Israel (Daniel 12:1). At the head of this great hierarchy are those angels who have the rank of archangel (Jude 9). And the greatest of all at the beginning, it seems, was one called Lucifer.

Almost all of what we know specifically about Satan's origin has to be worked out from two passages of Scripture. The first is in Ezekiel 28:12-19 and speaks allegorically about the king of Tyre. The second is in Isaiah 14:12-17. The name Lucifer means "son of the morning". He was the model of created perfection. He is described in the Ezekiel scripture as:

- being "full of wisdom";
- being "perfect in beauty"; and
- having the highest responsibility as "the anointed cherub".

Satan's Fall

We don't know how long this state of sinlessness lasted; but then came sin. And it began, not with the lowest of the creation of God, but with Lucifer, for Ezekiel 28 tells us that:

- his wisdom was corrupted;
- his beauty gave rise to pride in his heart; and
- he became no longer satisfied with his mighty position under God.

It's extremely significant that the root cause of this first sin was pride. We don't fully know what started it, or why God allowed it. Lucifer had been blameless, but now wickedness was found in him. It was the wickedness of pride - of self-centeredness. God said of him: "You said in your heart, 'I will ascend to the heavens; I will raise my throne above the stars of God; I will sit enthroned on the mount of assembly, on the utmost heights of Mount Zaphon. I will ascend above the tops of the clouds; I will make myself like the Most High'" (Isaiah 14:13-14).

Perhaps we can get an insight into this momentous event by contrasting Satan with Jesus as God the Son. He was, and is, superior to all angels (Hebrews 1:4, 6). God the Father, according to His eternal purpose, has appointed Him to become heir of all things (Hebrews 1:2). We don't know how much of this eternal purpose Lucifer knew about, but Lucifer certainly coveted the position and authority of Deity. So, being a created angel, he intended to exalt himself to become as God. He was therefore cast down (Luke 10:18) under the judgement of God - the inevitable result of pride (1 Timothy 3:6).

What a contrast to the Lord Jesus who, being God, humbled Himself to become lower than the angels (Hebrews 2:9) and so was exalted by God (Philippians 2:9)! "For all those who exalt themselves will be humbled, and those who humble themselves will be exalted" (Luke 18:14).

The Result of Satan's Fall

Often, in the ways of God, there is both an immediate and a future result. For example, in the case of our salvation, we are born again now and are immediately free from the penalty of sin - but we are not freed from the presence of sin until we leave this body. It is the same with Lucifer's sin. Pride and self-centeredness cannot exist for a moment in the presence of God.

For Lucifer, judgement ensued (Ezekiel 28:16) which Christ Himself witnessed (Luke 10:18). He was no longer Lucifer but "Satan" (i.e. the adversary) and "the devil" (i.e. the deceiver). And so the age-long conflict between the Creator and the greatest of His created beings, now sadly corrupted, had begun. It was to involve many hosts of the angels, it was to involve the entire human race and it was to involve the very Son of God.

It seems that Satan was not alone in his revolt but was in fact the leader of a great multitude of the spirit beings. Ephesians 6:12 speaks of "the spiritual forces of evil in the heavenly realm" and Jude 6 refers to "angels who did not keep their positions of authority" and are kept for future judgement. Thus Satan has his own angels - those demons who were so active during Christ's lifetime on this earth (Matthew 12:26).

During his temptation of Jesus in the wilderness, Satan claimed that all the authority and glory of the kingdoms of the world had been delivered to him (Luke 4:6). He has enormous power, for even the archangel Michael would not rebuke him (Jude 9). So Satan's domain is the earth (Revelation 2:13) and the air (Ephesians 2:2). Until the time of his future judgement, God allows him to exercise power, so that God's purposes may be completed. And so Satan still has access to God (see Job 1; Zechariah 3:1).

"We know that...the whole world is under the control of the evil one." (1 John 5:19). For Satan and his angels there is no repentance. Christ did not come to save angels but mankind (Hebrews 2:14-18). And so Satan is relentless in his opposition to God and to His purposes for the human race. Satan is still determined to be "as the Most High", to "ascend into heaven", and "to exalt his throne above the stars of God". Will he ever succeed? Read on and find out!

Battle Quotes 2

Satan has in fact a plan against the saints of the Most High which is to wear them out. What is meant by this phrase, "wear out"? It has in it the idea of reducing a little this minute, then reducing a little further the next minute. Reduce a little today, reduce a little tomorrow. Thus the wearing out is almost imperceptible; nevertheless, it is a reducing. The wearing down is scarcely an activity of which one is conscious, yet the end result is that there is nothing left. He will take away your prayer life little by little, and cause you to trust God less and less and yourself more and more, a little at a time. He will make you feel somewhat cleverer than before. Step by step, you are misled to rely more on your own gift, and step by step your heart is enticed away from the Lord. Now, were Satan to strike the children of God with great force at one time, they would know exactly how to resist the enemy since they would immediately recognize his work. He uses the method of gradualism to wear down the people of God. (Watchman Nee)

"We are evidently no friends of Satan. Like the kings of this world, he wars not against his own subjects. The very fact that he assaults us should fill our minds with hope." (JC Ryle)

10 PAUL'S BATTLE – WILD BEASTS AT EPHESUS (MARTIN JONES)

When we talk about the battle of the Christian, we don't usually think of physical combat in a literal sense. But there is a very curious verse that seems to indicate that Paul got himself involved in such a thing - and it is a verse that has caused great debate among Bible scholars for centuries: "If I fought wild beasts in Ephesus with no more than human hopes, what have I gained? If the dead are not raised, 'Let us eat and drink, for tomorrow we die'" (1 Corinthians 15:32).

The purpose of this chapter is to explore what Paul may have meant when he talked about fighting wild beasts and then, more importantly, explore why Paul was talking about wild beasts in the first place. There is something here that is key to apply to our own spiritual battle - but more of that later. So, fighting with wild beasts were you, Paul? Literally, or figuratively, may we ask? And, if figurative, who, or what were you talking about?

Option 1 – Persecuted in the Arena

This option believes that Paul really did fight wild beasts at Ephesus. If you are like me, you may be surprised to know that there are a number of learned people who take this view. Historically, it is not impossible that the event really did happen. There was a large arena at Ephesus which could well have seen gladiatorial combat and fights with wild beasts. We know from history that many Christians went to their death in such places under great persecution and in the most horrifying of circumstances. There are also some quite intriguing verses that could be interpreted as referring to such an event:

"But the Lord stood at my side and gave me strength, so that through me the message might be fully proclaimed and all the Gentiles might hear it. And I was delivered from the lion's mouth. The Lord will rescue me from every evil attack and will bring me safely to his heavenly kingdom. To him be glory for ever and ever. Amen" (2 Timothy 4:17-18).

"For it seems to me that God has put us apostles on display at the end of the procession, like those condemned to die in the arena. We have been made a spectacle to the whole universe, to angels as well as to human beings" (1 Corinthians 4:9).

"We do not want you to be uninformed, brothers and sisters, about the troubles we experienced in the province of Asia. We were under great pressure, far beyond our ability to endure, so that we despaired of life itself. Indeed, we felt we had received the sentence of death. But this happened that we might not rely on ourselves but on God, who raises the dead. He has delivered us from such a deadly peril, and he will deliver us again. On him we have set our hope that he will continue to deliver us" (2 Corinthians 1:8-10).

Was Paul referring to this incident in the above verses or would that be reading something into it that simply isn't there? Well, many believe that it is highly unlikely that Paul actually fought wild beasts in Ephesus and there are at least three reasons that can be put forward:

1) Paul most likely would not have survived it to be able to tell the tale! Even if you have watched the film "Gladiator", you will know that the survival rate for gladiators was very, very small – and these were

63

trained warriors. Paul was, by historical accounts, small, bow-legged and with an unimpressive physique – although used to working with his hands as a tent-maker, we have no evidence that he was skilled with weaponry. He could, of course, have been miraculously delivered out of the mouths of wild beasts just as happened to Daniel. But see the next points...

2) If it did really happen, it is very odd that he doesn't recount it along with his other sufferings and hardships in 2 Corinthians 11:23-29. Luke makes no mention of it in Acts either which would also be strange - but of course an argument from silence is not the strongest.

3) If he had been thrown to the beasts, it is said that he would automatically have lost his Roman citizenship - but we know from the Book of Acts that he still held it when he went before Caesar.

So a real event cannot probably be ruled out, but perhaps the most likely scenario is that if Paul was really referring to wild beasts, he meant it in a rhetorical sense - "if" I had fought wild beasts...

Option 2 – People of Ephesus

The mob scene described in Acts 19 has elements which remind you of a herd of wild beasts! Paul was teaching publicly that hand-made images of Greek gods were not gods, but false idols. This teaching especially annoyed the Ephesian artisans because the temple of Artemis was there and they made a profit from creating and selling gold and silver statues and other religious artifacts. In the scene in Acts 19, the city is enraged and several of Paul's Christian traveling companions are dragged into the midst of a mob; many of that mob had no idea why they were there! They had simply got caught up in it all – Paul's fellow-soldiers must have felt like they were in the middle of a herd of stampeding buffalo and that they could be squashed flat or torn limb from limb at any moment.

The drawback with this argument seems to be that Paul didn't fight with them, either metaphorically or literally. He was taken out of that situation for his own safety. Of course this was not the only time that he was at risk from a mob during his missionary career – it was one of those occupational hazards.

Option 3 – Philosophers

The third option is that Paul is referring to some philosophers who opposed him when he contended for the gospel. We don't have the space to go into a lot of detail about one bunch of philosophers who were known as the Epicureans - so you can do your own research. But it was the Epicureans who came from the "Let us eat and drink, for tomorrow we die" school of thought. To put it another way, they were in favour of a pretty hedonistic lifestyle because this life was all that they had.

The drawback to this theory is trying to understand exactly why Paul would have called these people "wild beasts" – it is possible that their philosophy gave them a license to live wild, uncontrolled lives that gave into "animalistic behaviour."

Option 4 – Principalities and Powers

Others see the wild beasts as a reference to the evil spirits, or "beasts", at work in the demon-possessed, the sorcerers and the idolaters of the city. In Jewish apocalyptic circles, the Greek word translated here as "beasts" was commonly used in reference to evil spirits and supernatural monsters. This connects with referring to demons as wild animals, a practice that Paul may well have encountered in Ephesus.

We know that folk religion, syncretism, magic and mystery cults were pervasive in 1st-century Asia Minor. In fact, Ephesus itself was known to be an epicenter of magic, witchcraft arts and the cult of Artemis - one of the major Greek goddesses known, amongst other things, as the Lady of the Beasts, the bull goddess and the huntress. As a huntress, she is said to have traveled in woods in the company of dogs, wild beasts and mountain nymphs – plenty of wild beast links here!

Paul's ministry here was filled with exorcisms and power encounters (see Acts 19) and Paul's own letter to the Ephesians reminds us that our"...struggle is not against flesh and blood, but against the rulers, against the authorities, against the powers of this dark world" (Ephesians 6:12). Further evidence may be taken from the grotesque fact that evil spirits in magic were often summoned through the images and organs of wild animals. Also, in Daniel and Revelation, we see beasts used to describe massive spiritual opposition to God's people. Finally, we see the devil is described in 1 Peter as a "roaring lion, seeking someone to devour" (1 Peter 5:8). The evidence is certainly intriguing but not conclusive.

Option 5 – Passions

It appears that since Plato, and at least up until the time of Paul's writing, "fighting the wild beasts" was euphemistic for struggling with human passions and especially those of a sexual nature. In particular, the philosopher, Dio Chrysostom described lusts as "savage beasts" which had to be destroyed and he noted that if this was not done thoroughly they would soon overwhelm and destroy. Was Paul using the phrase euphemistically to spare the blushes of his readers? Certainly, we know that Ephesus was rife with sexual immorality. The temple of Diana was populated with hordes of prostitutes associated with the temple worship – but it is perhaps hard for us to see someone as mature as Paul being enticed by such an apparently obvious temptation. We know that Paul spoke of these passions in relations to marriage:

"Now to the unmarried and the widows I say: It is good for them to stay unmarried, as I do. But if they cannot control themselves, they should marry, for it is better to marry than to burn with passion" (1 Corinthians 7:8-9).

It could be argued that if Paul had a particular issue with sexual temptation, he would have followed his own advice on marrying (assuming, of course, that he could find someone willing to take him on!) but the theory cannot be discounted entirely.

What is the message for us today?

Whatever Paul meant by "fighting with wild beasts", it would be a travesty if we missed the major point that he was trying to make in this chapter. The key to this passage is understanding the role of the resurrection – this theme was at the forefront of Paul's mind when he was writing to the Corinthians from Ephesus. All of 1 Corinthians 15 is devoted to the hope of the bodily resurrection of believers in Jesus Christ and his atoning sacrifice on the cross. Why did Paul fight with wild beasts? There was only an advantage to it because of one thing – the amazing reality that his body was going to be resurrected to eternal life. What do we need to remember constantly?

- There will be eternal consequences of the battle that we are fighting here on the earth. There should be no such thing for the Christian as simply "living in the moment."
- Our main priority in life is not simply to make ourselves comfort-able and enjoy the pleasures of life while we can. But nor is the Christian's life all about defeating each day's beasts (whatever form they may take for us as individuals); it's about the bigger

picture - our identity and life, both today and eternally, which is given meaning and power through the empty tomb.

- There is still something to be fighting for. "Eat and drink, for tomorrow we die" is the talk of fatalists, but it is also the talk of the defeated. The phrase Paul uses is taken from Isaiah 22:13, referring to the Jews who were besieged by Sennacherib and the army of the Assyrians. The prophet says that instead of weeping, fasting and humiliation, as they should have been doing in those circumstances, they had given themselves up to feasting and revelry. They had come to the conclusion that there was no use in offering resistance to the enemy, or in calling upon God for His help – it was too late and there was nothing that could be done now. Paul never gave up the fight until the day he died and neither should we, no matter how tough the battle gets and how much that defeat seems to be the only outcome. The empty tomb should remind us that, actually, the battle is already won.

Battle Thoughts

The Upward Calling of God

Fellow-disciple, are you aiming for the prize of the upward calling of God in Christ Jesus? If so, then you must guard your soul. No one else can guard it for you. Look out for the things that war against the soul. Stand clear! Whatever the cost...

The prize of the upward calling of God is too valuable a thing to be frittered away for some earthly pleasure. Take up your cross and follow Christ. Crucify the flesh with its passions and lusts. This world's dark hour calls for men mighty in prayer and faith; men who refuse to yield to the lust of the flesh, the lust of the eyes, and the vanity of life. Take your place with these men and count all things as rubbish for the excellency of the knowledge of Christ Jesus your Lord. (Guy Jarvie)

Heeding the Call

In these easy-going days don't we need to examine again what part we are playing in this great conflict? The powers of darkness are directed against us as individuals and against us in our assembly life. Some, through their own negligence, get disabled in the battle. Wounded soldiers are not only eliminated from the conflict, they also become a drain on others, and absorb energies which should be directed against the common foe. Some appear to have retired from the conflict and have become mere on-lookers. They leave others to do the fighting, but reserve themselves the right to criticize. The need for saints to take up the whole armour of God was never more urgent than it is today. Shall we not heed the call? "Be on your guard; stand firm in the faith; be courageous; be strong" (1 Corinthians 16:13). (Tom Hyland)

11 THE HIDDEN BATTLE - THE ACCUSER (LINDSAY PRASHER)

How often have we heard from gospel preachers that heaven is a place where no sin can enter? While this is true of the eternal state (Revelation 22:3, 15), Ephesians 6:12 speaks of "spiritual forces of evil in the heavenly realms." You can't escape the conclusion that, in God's infinite wisdom, He allows access by forces of evil into the heavenlies - and there are examples of Satan approaching right into God's presence.

Accusing the High Priest

One example occurs in Zechariah chapter 3, where the prophet's fourth vision is recounted. He sees Joshua the High Priest of Israel standing in filthy clothes before an angel of God. The angel is told to replace the dirty garments with clean ones. The reason is not hard to find. The visions followed the end of the seventy years of captivity in Babylon and the return to worship in God's re-built temple in Jerusalem. In this vision the prophet was being prepared for the re-establishment of divine worship after the long lapse. It is against this backdrop that Satan is seen standing as an opponent right beside the angel and, as the voice of God was heard by the prophet directly addressing the adversary, it would appear that the scene is set in heaven. Satan was out to stop the return to the true worship if he could.

However, God stepped in and in effect told Satan that he had fuelled the fire of departure of God's people long enough, but He had pulled out of the fire this burning stick and quenched it. God said that, though Joshua's clothes were dirty, they had now been made clean to serve Him in His new house in Jerusalem and nothing Satan could do would reverse it. Just as Satan did his best to prevent the return to collective worship according to the Law of Moses, which applied in Old Testament times, so today in New Testament times he endeavours to thwart collective worship in the house of God.

Accusing Believers

Another example of Satan's activity before God affects Christians as individuals, rather than their collective life, for in Revelation 12:10 our adversary is devastatingly described as the accuser of the brothers. This implies that when you or I do wrong things, Satan goes to God and draws attention to what we have done, asking whether God will own us when we do such things. So we must all be careful not to give our enemy the chance to run to God and point the accusing finger at us.

The amazing feature of this situation is that, despite such accusation, if we are really sorry for our sin and tell God so, God will forgive us in His wonderful mercy. But how much better not to fall into wrong-doing in the first place, then we don't give our ruthless foe the opportunity which he relishes.

Accusing a Faithful Man

A third and outstanding example of Satan's action in God's presence is found in the story of Job. You might think that, because Job was so upright and blameless and because he shunned evil, the adversary would have nothing to point the finger at. Yet such is the subtlety of Satan, his attack took the following line. He told God that it was easy for Job to be faithful because he had been given so many comforts and blessings. If these were removed, he would curse God to His face.

Fully knowing what He was doing, God gave Satan permission to take away all Job's possessions, but not to touch the man himself. The story is well known; how his cattle and their herdsmen, his sheep and their shepherds, his camels and their attendants and even his sons and daughters were all killed in turn. Job didn't sin or charge God with foolishness in all this. The relentless foe did not stop at that. He appeared before God a second time and said: "'Skin for skin!' Satan replied. 'A man will give all he has for his own life. But now stretch out your hand and strike his flesh and bones, and he will surely curse you to your face'" (Job 2:4-5).

So God again allowed Satan to do what he wished except that Job's life must be spared. At this Satan caused boils to erupt all over Job's body. However, even when his wife said, "Curse God and die!" Job's reply was, "Shall we accept good from God, and not trouble?" So the real trust that Job had in God shone out more strongly because of his terrible misfortunes and Satan's ploys were foiled.

Instinctively we turn the spotlight from Job to ourselves and have to recognize that God allows Satan to make Christians suffer at times to some degree. The degree may vary from person to person, but what a comfort it is to know that God will not let you be tested beyond what you can bear and will always provide a way out so that you can endure it (1 Corinthians 10:13). What this tells us is that Job must have been outstandingly strong spiritually or else God would not have allowed Satan to tempt him so much.

There was only one really perfect Man who totally pleased God, and, while there is no record of Satan appearing before God in relation to the Lord Jesus, we do know he tempted Him at every turn; directly as during the forty days in the wilderness and indirectly through the action of men under the Devil's sway, culminating in the crucifixion at Calvary. Yet Calvary was the scene of Christ's triumph through suffering infinitely greater than Job's. Jesus gave up the spirit with the resounding cry, "It is finished". The adversary had certainly bruised the heel of the Seed of the woman as God forecast to Adam and Eve – but he himself received a head blow as Genesis 3 had foretold.

The truth of this was seen on the resurrection morning, when the Scripture reveals that, not only was His body raised from the tomb, but His soul left Sheol, taking captivity captive, having the keys of death and Hades formerly held by the adversary. This is a good point at which to complete the Job story, for God repaid the man who suffered so much under the hand of Satan, by giving him twice as much as he had before and blessed him with seven more sons and three more daughters, the fairest in all the land. So Christ, by His victory over Satan, at whose hand He suffered so much more, will be more than satisfied to see around His throne thousands who will be beautiful in His glory.

You and I can look forward to being among them. Praise His Name!

The A-Z of Satan – D to K

- Deceiver/Dragon – "The great dragon was hurled down – that ancient serpent called the devil, or Satan, who leads the whole world astray. He was hurled to the earth, and his angels with him" (Revelation 12:9).
- Devil – "...what is sinful is of the devil, because the devil has been sinning from the beginning. The reason the Son of God appeared was to destroy the devil's work" (1 John 3:8).
- Enemy – "...and the enemy who sows them is the devil. The harvest is the end of the age, and the harvesters are angels" (Matthew 13:39)
- Evil one – "My prayer is not that you take them out of the world but that you protect them from the evil one" (John 17:15)
- Father of lies – "You belong to your father, the devil, and you want to carry out your father's desires. He was a murderer from the beginning, not holding to the truth, for there is no truth in him. When he lies, he speaks his native language, for he is a liar and the father of lies" (John 8:44).
- God of this age – "The god of this age has blinded the minds of unbelievers, so that they cannot see the light of the gospel that displays the glory of Christ..." (2 Corinthians 4:4).
- King of Babylon – "You will take up this taunt against the king of Babylon: How the oppressor has come to an end! How his fury has ended!" (Isaiah 14:4).
- King of Tyre – "Son of man, take up a lament concerning the king

of Tyre and say to him: 'This is what the Sovereign Lord says: "You were the seal of perfection, full of wisdom and perfect in beauty'" (Ezekiel 28:12).

12 ISRAEL'S BATTLE – JERICHO AND AI (NEVILLE COOMER)

Trusting and obeying leads to victory

Jericho was taken, its walls fell flat and the battle ended in complete victory for God's people. What was the secret of their great success? If we can learn how God's earthly people won their battles it may help us to be overcomers today. Joshua had this word from the Lord: "See, I have delivered Jericho into your hands, along with its king and its fighting men." Then the Lord set out the plan of campaign. Joshua and all the people trusted in God, believed His word and totally obeyed His instructions. Once every day for six days they walked around the city wall in silence. They persevered in something which to the natural eye must have appeared ridiculous. But their obedience to God's word was the secret of their success. On the seventh day they shouted and the walls fell. Israel proved the truth of Rahab's words to the two spies, "the Lord your God is God in heaven above and on the earth below."

Over-confidence in own strength brings defeat

The story of Ai is a different one: the battle ended in defeat. Jericho's fall brought fame to Joshua, but Ai was a humbling experience. Why this failure at Ai after the success at Jericho? The spies sent to find out the size and state of Ai returned to Joshua with the report: "When they returned to Joshua, they said, 'Not all the army will have to go up against Ai. Send two or three thousand men to take it and do not weary the whole army, for only a few people live there'" (Joshua 7:3).

This time Joshua did not ask God but did what the spies suggested. He grossly under-estimated the enemy's strength and the men of Israel were put to flight before the men of Ai. In our spiritual conflict we should never under-estimate the strength of the enemy and we should always seek God's face in prayer. If God is with us, who can stand against us? On this occasion God was not with Joshua and his men because of sin among the people. One man sinned, yet all were affected, and so they suffered defeat. Should we not ask ourselves - is there anything in my life that may be holding back victory from God's people? "For none of us lives for ourselves alone, and none of us dies for ourselves alone" (Romans 14:7).

The spies counselled Joshua not to make the whole army work but the victory at Jericho was not gained by work but by faith, and without faith it is impossible to please God (Hebrews 11:6). When failure occurs, there should be self-examination, and where there is wrong it should be corrected. It's only then that we can expect God to give us the victory. After Achan had been dealt with, Joshua prayed to the Lord and received the answer of guaranteed success: "...Do not be afraid; do not be discouraged. Take the whole army with you, and go up and attack Ai. For I have delivered into your hands the king of Ai, his people, his city and his land. You shall do to Ai and its king as you did to Jericho and its king..." (Joshua 8:1-2). Success is sure if God is with us. But we must always act on the word of God, and be in a right spiritual condition to gain the victory. "I can do all this through him who gives me strength", wrote Paul to the Philippians. When Ai had been totally destroyed, Joshua built an altar to the Lord. Our worship and praise, too, should flow as we experience the power of Almighty God with us in our lives. "...for the Lord your God is God in heaven above and on the earth below" (Joshua 2:11).

Battle Quotes 3

"Don't be surprised if there is an attack on your work, on you who are called to do it, on your innermost nature - the hidden person of the heart. It must be so. The great thing is not to be surprised, nor to count it strange - for that plays into the hand of the enemy. Is it possible that anyone should set himself to exalt our beloved Lord and not instantly become a target for many arrows? The very fact that our work depends utterly on Him and can't be done for a moment without Him calls for a very close walk and a constant communion of spirit. This alone is enough to account for anything the enemy can do. Don't be surprised if you suffer. It is part of the way of the cross...So rejoice! You are giving Him what He asks you to give Him: the chance to show you what He can do." (Amy Carmichael)

"Just as lilies bloom white in cess pools, so human virtues have reached unparalleled beauty amid the horrors of war. It need not surprise us that as an image to convey the nature of Christian living, the Holy Spirit uses that of warfare. No image can be more apt." (John White)

13 THE BATTLE FOR...THE SOUL (MARTIN JONES)

Target – Salvation

Has it ever occurred to you that there are an awful lot of people out there who don't believe they have a soul? They freely admit that they have a body (obviously), which starts off bald, wrinkly, seems unable to control bodily functions and, sooner or later, usually ends up that way as well. No arguments here.

Then of course there is the "spirit", which might be seen as the life which makes the body work that disappears on death. Some might believe that the spirit simply returns back to being part of "Mother Nature." And that is pretty much it - two-dimensional and totally temporary. Life basically boils down to a few litres of water, salts and some fairy dust to make it all happen – and when you die, it's all over. "Eat, drink and be merry, for tomorrow we die" or, as Jon Bon Jovi once put it "I'll live while I'm alive and sleep when I'm dead."

Our first reaction might be "if it only it were so simple." But - when we really think about it – "thank God that it's not." Wise old Solomon gave us a mini-lesson in theo-biology when he said in Ecclesiastes "and the dust returns to the ground it came from, and the spirit returns to God who gave it." But that doesn't give us the full story because Paul gives us the third dimension in 1 Thessalonians 5:23: "...May your whole spirit, soul and body be kept blameless at the coming of our Lord Jesus Christ."

Leaving the difficult question of how our spirits can be kept blameless for another day, what is this soul of which Paul speaks? You would think with about 94 other references to this word in the NIV translation of the Bible, it wouldn't be hard to define. But reading most of them probably doesn't get us too far, except that it becomes clear that the soul is connected with feeling – it can feel weariness, joy, grief, love, praise, longing and other things as well. You can make a study of it yourself. But what exactly is it?

It is just as well that David was well in touch with his soul because he gives us a vital clue in Psalm 103:1: "Praise the LORD, my soul; all my inmost being, praise his holy name." There was a little device in ancient poetry where the poet would say the same thing twice but in a slightly different way. It seems a bit odd to us now, but what it tells us is that David saw his soul as his "inmost being." To put it another way, it was what made David, David. It is one of Satan's greatest and most effective lies – that man is simply body and spirit. It's wrong on so many levels:

i) it reduces man to the same level as the rest of God's creation, supporting the lie that we evolved from more primitive life forms;

ii) it forces either an undue focus on the body because that is all life is about, or neglect/abuse of the body because it has no meaning connected to it or long-term purpose; and

iii) it completely ignores the fact that there is a supernatural war being waged by God and Satan – not over man's body or spirit, but over his very soul.

Jesus, as usual, put His finger right on the button when He said: "Do not be afraid of those who kill the body but cannot kill the soul. Rather, be afraid of the One who can destroy both soul and body in hell" (Matthew 10:28). He was talking about Himself, of course, in the role of Judge. It is a very worrying state of affairs, to put it mildly, when the people we know and love dearly neither believe in the existence of their own soul, nor the existence of the One who can determine the eternal destiny of it, or the one who would be so diabolically delighted to see their soul condemned to hell with him.

But let's unpack what the problem is here. Ezekiel 18 puts it pretty bluntly for us doesn't it? "The soul who sins is the one who will die." We might think of this as physical death, which is certainly true, in a sense – that was a consequence of the Fall that we now all have to face. But Revelation 2:11 speaks of another type of death: "...The one who is victorious will not be hurt at all by the second death." Revelation 20 tells us that "the lake of fire is the second death."

What the lake of fire signifies is dealt with elsewhere in this Anthology, but let's just focus on the point for now that it involves eternal and permanent separation from God and where the soul that experiences feelings will be in a state of torment caused by its' current predicament. It really is too awful to think about for too long - yet we must, for this will spur us on to greater witness. There is a present aspect to the battle for the soul though, which we mustn't lose sight of. We sometimes speak about the future consequences of not believing and of time running out to make a decision to become a follower of Jesus and accept his offer of salvation. This is all true; but let's not forget that unbelievers are experiencing spiritual death right now, as Paul told the church in Ephesus:

"...you were dead in your transgressions and sins, in which you used to live when you followed the ways of this world and of the ruler of the kingdom of the air, the spirit who is now at work in those who are disobedient. All of us also lived among them at one time, gratifying the cravings of our flesh and following its desires and thoughts. Like the rest, we were by nature deserving of wrath" (Ephesians 2:1-3).

Isn't it sobering to think that when we look at our friends who do not believe - and may appear to be quite happy and content in that fact, totally unconcerned that they are separated from God and that they do not know Him or care to have a relationship with Him - we are looking at a spiritual corpse. To use an imperfect analogy, we're looking into the face of someone suffering with an advanced form of cancer who, unless dramatic surgery intervenes very soon, is going to be consumed so totally with this disease that it is beyond cure. The analogy breaks in the sense that death has already occurred, but is wonderfully superceded by the amazing fact that God wants to bring every human being back from the dead to eternal life – life that is characterised by, and based on, a right relationship with Him. Jesus Himself recognized that this life-giving process was not going to come cheap: "What good is it for someone to gain the whole world, yet forfeit their soul? Or what can anyone give in exchange for their soul?" (Mark 8:36-37).

Psalm 49:8 agrees: "the ransom for a life is costly, no payment is ever enough..." This was true as far as earthly payment was concerned, but the divine payment of God's own Son, was, thankfully, enough. This was God's great battle strategy for the soul – in fact His only strategy. There was, and is, no plan B. No-one comes to the Father except through Jesus.

Enemy Strategy

Unlike God, Satan could not, and cannot, adopt a "one-size fits all" strategy in the battle for the soul; his cannot be a "Shock and Awe" approach for he lacks the firepower. He has to be far more subtle. There are a myriad of options at his disposal which he uses skilfully to steer people away from this matter of the eternal destiny of their souls. Here are just three of the most common approaches:

- Denial – Satan encourages people to defiantly refuse to believe in the concept of sin generally, and applying to them personally, the existence of God and the need for salvation.
- Delay – He distracts people and puts them off thinking deeply about these issues until another day so that many end up never making a salvation decision at all. But of course, making no decision is a default "No" decision.
- Doubt – The adversary plants seeds of doubt in people in areas like the mechanics of salvation (how can this work – don't I need to work for it?), the problem of suffering in the world, other barriers to faith, whether they are too bad to be saved, or are truly saved.

Defence Mechanisms

Ways to combat Satan's attacks include:

- Effective apologetics (basically giving a reason for the hope that is within us) – many Christians feel ill-equipped in this area. They have accepted the Christian message, potentially assisted by the efforts of others, but find it difficult to answer tough questions themselves. Apologetics might be theological in nature but can also cover such areas as physics, geology, astronomy, biology, philosophy, archaeology, philology to name a few. The answers are out there but it takes time and effort to research, investigate and compile adequate arguments. A simple testimony of the thought process that led you to salvation can be equally, or even more, powerful in the absence of detailed answers.

- Christian lifestyle witness – unfortunately Satan can use the lifestyle of Christians as a barrier to salvation, when a worldly lifestyle can lead to accusations of hypocrisy or conclusions that salvation has no effect. On the other hand, the lifestyle of an active Christian can be an attractive and powerful testimony to the unbeliever.
- Preaching – it is tempting these days to shy away from preaching and hope that lifestyle testimony is sufficient. However, lifestyle witness is generally the means to open up the possibility of the person being receptive to the preaching and is not an end in itself. As Paul said, how will people believe if no-one tells them? This is where there is no substitute for knowledge of the message of the Bible overall and specific key verses which the Holy Spirit can bring to your mind at just the right time to convict the hearer of their need for salvation.

We can truly thank God that it can be said to us that "...you are receiving the end result of your faith, the salvation of your souls" (1 Peter 1:9). Our prayer is that the same will be said of the people that God brings us into contact with.

Powerful Prayer (Guy Jarvie)

"What can we do?" We must pray, for power comes through prayer. The prayer of faith can still move mountains of difficulties. And isn't God's word like a hammer that breaks the rock into pieces? But effective prayer begins in secret: it doesn't begin in the prayer meeting.

"But when you pray, go into your room, close the door and pray to your Father, who is unseen. Then your Father, who sees what is done in secret, will reward you" (Matthew 6:6).

Prayer all alone! That is the beginning of power. Praying for others; praying for power to love, to serve, to preach. Secret prayer and praise and thanksgiving are essential to spiritual power. When prayer in secret is scanty or absent then our collective prayer in prayer meetings becomes weak and powerless. When our prayer meetings become formal and without the clear leading of the Holy Spirit, then the cause is evident - we have failed to seek God earnestly behind the shut door, our private prayer has been lacking. Only the moving of the Spirit of God in our hearts will bring reviving to our souls, and only the convicting power of the Spirit will break the stony hearts of men around us.

Brothers and sisters, let us bow our knees to the Father who sees in secret. Let us supplicate Him for the grace and power without which we cannot prevail in the spiritual conflict. Then when we gather for collective prayer and praise, great grace and power will be upon us, and walls of indifference will breakdown before us. "Jesus Christ is the same yesterday and today and forever." What He has been to others in the past He can be to us today.

14 PAUL'S BATTLE – THE MAGICIANS (MARTIN JONES)

"Some Jews who went around driving out evil spirits tried to invoke the name of the Lord Jesus over those who were demon-possessed. They would say, "In the name of the Jesus whom Paul preaches, I command you to come out." Seven sons of Sceva, a Jewish chief priest, were doing this. One day the evil spirit answered them, "Jesus I know, and Paul I know about, but who are you?" Then the man who had the evil spirit jumped on them and overpowered them all. He gave them such a beating that they ran out of the house naked and bleeding.

When this became known to the Jews and Greeks living in Ephesus, they were all seized with fear, and the name of the Lord Jesus was held in high honor. Many of those who believed now came and openly confessed what they had done. A number who had practiced sorcery brought their scrolls together and burned them publicly. When they calculated the value of the scrolls, the total came to fifty thousand drachmas. In this way the word of the Lord spread widely and grew in power" (Acts 19:13-20).

As we've seen in another chapter, the apostle Paul had lots of physical battles in his life but he was no stranger to spiritual conflict either. In this case, we're not talking about doctrinal differences with the Pharisees or the Jews but a battle at a supernatural level. This chapter takes a look at the background to the story and then looks at four actions that occurred which have a real relevance to us today.

Background

Of all the hostile places that Paul visited, it is possible that Ephesus was top of his list – he encountered idolatry, demon possession and magic spells there and that was all in one chapter!

Ephesus is now in modern-day Turkey and a popular destination for cruise tourists, even though the harbour which made it a thriving port has long since silted up. It was a bit of a tourist attraction back then as well - mainly due to the existence of one of the seven wonders of the Ancient world, the Temple of Artemis. (If you live in Britain, you don't need to travel far to see it; more of the temple is now in the British museum than in Ephesus!)

The Ephesian Artemis was a mixture of the goddess of hunting & war and the goddess of fertility - and it must have been no coincidence that Ephesus was known for both idolatry and immorality. There was an idol of Artemis within her temple that was declared by tradition to have fallen from the sky. Upon it were inscribed symbolic characters, which were believed to possess great power. There is a story of an ancient wrestler (potentially an Olympian) who was said to have won successive bouts because he had some of these magic characters around his ankle. When they were discovered and removed – he lost! Books had been written by the Ephesians to explain the meaning and use of these symbols. It is possible that the books that got toasted that day were of this kind.

Quantify

A drachma was worth about a day's wages. The temple tax was 2 drachmas (Jesus provided a four drachma coin for him and Peter to use).

You would need to earn just short of 137 years to earn 50,000 drachmas. Why were they so expensive? At that time all books were precious; for they were made of skins instead of paper, and were pen-printed instead of printed by type. Magic books were especially high-priced because each owner was interested in restricting the information and so was unwilling to permit anyone to make a copy of his book. Viewed from this standpoint, the number of books would not necessarily have had to have been very great in order to amount to fifty thousand pieces of silver.

Simplify

On a very simple level, the former magicians recognized that they needed to simplify and take out the trash. At the time of writing, Amazon.com has over 800,000 Kindle books for sale and over 1.75 million hard copy books. Amazon.co.uk has 461,000 DVD's. You could use all manner of statistics to illustrate just how much "stuff" is out there. It is stuff that runs the whole scale of "harmful" to "beneficial". There are many other things that can fill our lives – sport, hobbies, culture, travel, vacations, politics, house and home. It is tempting to absorb yourself into it: acquiring stuff, signing up to do things, making commitments, making plans. A recent survey found that the average American child has 8 hours of screen time A DAY! And that is just the average. Boggling. The call to the Christian is simple – SIMPLIFY. Every January, companies fill their marketing brochures with two things – fitness machines and racking for your closet.

We need racking for our spiritual lives so that everything is put in its proper place and the junk is chucked out. If you find you don't have the time to read your Bible every day – you need to simplify. If you don't have time to pray to God every day – you need to simplify. If you find you cannot attend meetings or gatherings of saints on anything like a very regular and consistent basis – no prizes for guessing - you need to simplify.

"I consider my life worth nothing to me; my only aim is to finish the race and complete the task the Lord Jesus has given me—the task of testifying to the good news of God's grace" (Acts 20:24).

"What is more, I consider everything a loss because of the surpassing worth of knowing Christ Jesus my Lord, for whose sake I have lost all things. I consider them garbage, that I may gain Christ and be found in him" (Philippians 3:8).

"No one serving as a soldier gets entangled in civilian affairs, but rather tries to please his commanding officer" (2 Timothy 2:4).

Let us ask the Lord to put on our hearts what needs to be simplified in our lives so that we can focus wholeheartedly on serving him and to help us stop complicating our lives in future with peripheral stuff.

Crucify

As well as simplifying, we need to crucify. The former magicians give us a very good example of what this means in practice. They were convicted that it was not good for them to have these books. They could have chosen to simply decide not to look at them anymore. They could have promised to lock them away. They could have elected to sell them and earn a fantastic amount of money. But no – the only course of action that they felt they could take was to burn the books. It is said about crucifixion that the man going to the cross was never going to come back – it was permanent. Once the books were burned, there was no going back – they were irreplaceable. Think of the decommissioning process that happened in Northern Ireland a few years – weapons were "put beyond use." Paul had quite a lot to say about the old fashioned topic of "mortification":

"For we know that our old self was crucified with him so that the body ruled by sin might be done away with, that we should no longer be slaves to sin" (Romans 6:6).

"I have been crucified with Christ and I no longer live, but Christ lives in me. The life I now live in the body, I live by faith in the Son of God, who loved me and gave himself for me" (Galatians 2:20).

"Those who belong to Christ Jesus have crucified the flesh with its passions and desires" (Galatians 5:24).

The former magicians had broken free from their slavery to sin by taking permanent and radical action. Are there things in our lives that need the same ruthless treatment? Again, we need to pray that God will reveal this to us and ask him for the strength to take that step. Remember how you deal with an intruding bug in your home? You take as large an object as you can lift and batter the harmless creature until it is nothing more than pulp – and then you bash it again just to make sure.

Edify

The magicians realised that the books they had treasured were not edifying to them. In other words they were not doing them any good as Christians. They were not building them up. It is nice to speculate about what happened when they went back to their homes and saw the big space on the bookshelf were their old magic books had been. What did they fill the space with – the books of the old Testament, letters from Paul, editions of NT magazine? Whatever, we can imagine that they were now to be focused on things that were edifiying to them. What about us – of all the stuff that is on our shelves and in our heads – how much of it is edifying? There is so much excellent free Christian material out there (like on Youtube), it is quite possible to almost do away with TV altogether – if we switch our thinking from entertainment to edification and realise that being edified is actually "entertaining" in its own way. Let us ask God for help, through the Holy Spirit, to get weaned off junk and onto spiritual food whether it be milk or meat depending on the stage we're at.

"Finally, brothers and sisters, whatever is true, whatever is noble, whatever is right, whatever is pure, whatever is lovely, whatever is admirable - if anything is excellent or praiseworthy - think about such things" (Philippians 4:8).

Glorify

There is no doubt that God was glorified by what was done that day. In a sense it was almost as well pleasing to him as the Old Testament sacrifices – the meaning was different but the heart motive was there. It is easy to lose the focus of our lives which is to glorify God and bring honour to his name. Each can glorify God in his or her own situation. It would have been fantastic if the silversmiths had followed suit, later in the chapter, by melting down their idols and scrapping their machinery – but that wasn't to be. What was at the route of this glorification was pure and simple obedience to the Word of God. That applies to us today. Hear it – accept it – do it. We can wrap how we act in a whole range of excuses but in the end it all comes down to obedience.

Why?

· If we do all of these things we will feel fantastic. Being a Christian is not only about feelings of course, but we should have an underlying quality of feeling – a peace and joy that comes with knowing we are in the right place and doing what God wants us to do.

· It is the best way to be effective as a Christian. Feeling great is one thing, and there are other things in life that can attempt to replicate that. But if we say we are disciples of Jesus, surely our goal is to be the best disciple we can be? Anything less is really just playing at it, isn't it?

· God expects it and he deserves it. There was no direct command, as far as we know, for them to go and burn the books. But they seem to have immediately recognized what was required of them and they got on and did it. Even Demetrius figured out that the Christians believed in only one God – every other allegiance had to go out of the window. You may not find a specific Bible verse to start doing A or stop doing B but deep in your heart, God will place a conviction into you that you must do it. It is ever so important that we listen to God when he is speaking to us. If we do not then our hearts get a little bit harder each time we don't.

· We want God to bless us, individually and as a church. What does that look like? Acts 19 goes on to say the "Word spread and spread in power." We want to see God's power at work don't we – in people being saved, in disciples growing, in the church being vibrant? May God help us to do our part so that He will do His part.

I May Never March....

I may never march in the infantry
Ride in the cavalry
Shoot with the artillery
I may never zoom o'er the enemy
But I'm in the Lord's army!

I'm in the Lord's army! (Yes, Sir!)
I'm in the Lord's army! (Yes, Sir)

In the name of Jesus
In the name of Jesus,
In the name of Jesus
We have the victory,
In the name of Jesus,
In the name of Jesus
Demons will have to flee,
When we stand on the name of Jesus
Tell me who can stand before,
In the mighty name of Jesus,
We have the victory.

15 BATTLE ROUND 2 – SATAN V ADAM & EVE (GEOFF HYDON)

The Serpent

The principal characteristic of Satan is found in his name, which originally meant adversary. In his opposition to God and man we first find him described as the Serpent. This title is confined mainly to the books of Genesis and Revelation and is usually linked to his work as the arch-deceiver (Genesis 3; Revelation 12:9; 20:10). In this, his character is the complete opposite of God who cannot lie (Hebrews 6:18).

We could speculate that the subtle character of the serpent led Satan to choose that creature for his physical presence in Eden, but Scripture doesn't record whether that choice was made solely by the evil one or with the permission of God (compare Matthew 8:32). Nor does it explain the ability of the serpent to communicate effectively with the woman. As a general scriptural principle, we are expected simply to exercise faith in what God has seen fit to record of the matter.

One thing is clear from that record: the fall of man was designed and prompted by the wily intervention of the Deceiver in God's perfect creation. So, the Serpent was allowed to bring the spiritual power play of evil against good into the realm of mankind.

The Scene

The effects of the Serpent's work in the Garden of Eden can only be judged properly when account is taken of the original creation, which bore the seal of God's approval. Everything was good, both in terms of man's environment and, more importantly, of his relationship with God his Maker. All that man required to satisfy him: food and water, authority and companionship, were provided. Most important of all, communion with God was a privilege enjoyed by Adam and Eve. What a wonderful revelation of God's will and work they must have had! They viewed with sinless eyes the wonders of a perfect creation. The holy, all-powerful and loving character of God must have been even more clearly visible to them than the psalmist, who, despite the taint of sin could yet, in Psalm 19, witness to the magnificence of God's creation.

The Sin

Into this glorious scene comes the arch-deceiver, the Serpent, with a triple temptation to thoroughly "beguile" Eve (2 Corinthians 11:3). There is a subtle difference of degree between doubt and disbelief which is starkly brought before us in the account of the Fall in the contrast between the Serpent's words to Eve, "has God said?", and his further statement "you shall not surely die"; the latter containing the prompting simply to disbelieve. He first planted the doubt then suggested advantages if only Eve would disbelieve. In the same way we often are guided by his tricks to "just try", on the basis of doubts as to whether a course of action is really wrong. Which of us can point an accusing finger at Eve? In her case the Serpent's three-pronged attack was quickly completed when he prompted her, in view of the apparent benefits, to take the fruit.

1 John 2:16 has often been compared to Eve's response to the tempter; the lusts of the flesh,the eyes and the vainglory of life being linked to her view of the fruit as (i) food, (ii) a delight to look upon, and (iii) being desired to make her wise. How the course of our history would

have been changed if she had fed on God's food, looked away to view God's handiwork, and satisfied herself with the wisdom of doing His will! But her initial resistance to the Tempter soon melted away.

Maybe it was Adam who had told Eve not so much as to touch the fruit; he after all was the one to receive the command - even before Eve's creation. Perhaps the instruction was repeated directly by God to Eve. By whatever means she received the command, it was disastrously ignored.

1 Timothy 2:14 tells us that Adam wasn't beguiled like Eve. Based on the events that had taken place he simply had to decide, of his God-given freewill, his course of action. His sin was outright disobedience of the holy command - the result of his deliberate judgement.

The Sad Consequences

At that point the Serpent had apparently accomplished his objective. He had successfully struck at the whole of God's earthly creation by striking at its head - Adam. As Romans 5:12 tells us, the venom of his deadly bite would now pass to all earth's inhabitants causing death, which in man's case had a twofold aspect: a primary break in his relationship with God and a secondary spoiling of the physical harmony of man and his environment.

While rampant sin would soon have its disastrous effects, the initial changes resulted from the righteous judgements of God. The ideal surroundings of the Garden were put out of bounds. The ground was cursed, changing man's enjoyable labour to arduous toil. Mental and physical anguish began, as evidenced by Adam and Eve's hiding from God, and God's statement to Eve concerning childbirth.

Subsequently, man's dominion over the animal kingdom was disturbed; killing and being killed came to be parts of a new natural law of survival, and animals had to be put to death to meet the physical and spiritual needs of man. Death had entered the world and in its primary form it cut the links between man and God (as evidenced by the ejection from the Garden and the need for sacrifices in order to approach God from then on).

Clearly, God's pronouncement as to the punishment of death had wider significance than the cessation of Adam's heartbeat and respiration. Death in that physical sense was to occur much later, although the biological process of ageing immediately began. Physical obstacles to communion as a result of expulsion from the Garden were subsequent to a spiritual break in the relationship between Adam and God, which caused the man to hide from his Maker as a result of his sin. It is this spiritual "death" to which God was principally referring when giving Adam the command concerning the Tree of Knowledge. We may describe such a severe break in communion as death.

Consider for a moment what it is that first suggests to us the death of almost any living thing - it is the lack of response. We sense that something has occurred which has cut off all lines of communication and we describe that circumstance as death. So God said that Adam would die, in the sense of being separated spiritually from God and lacking in response to Him, even whilst his blood was still coursing through his veins. The root of the problem lay not in his heartbeat but in his heart condition, in the change of his very nature which ruled his attitude towards God. The sin which we see in ourselves today results from that change. Man had a God-given ability to decide either to obey or disobey the command of God and that ability has progressively been exercised in disobedience since the Fall.

Vigorous attempts by individuals and groups throughout history to prove that man can cleanse his character if his surroundings are improved have been doomed to failure because of the continuing work of the deceiver, who caused the basic change in man's nature to occur. When Satan struck at Adam he had in view not only changing Adam's nature and staining his character, but the marring of God's creation for all time.

How close he came to success because of the unstoppable transmission of sin by Adam to all his descendants! For surely we now take our characteristics from the fallen nature of Adam (see Romans 5:19; 1 Corinthians 15:22, 48). We now sin because we are born sinners (see Psalm 51:5; Romans 3:10; Ephesians 2:1). Death in Eden was so far-reaching. The effects on us of the Serpent's attack are awfully reflected in Galatians 5:19-21 where the term "the flesh" describes the fallen nature. As we see how a child's hands, once disobediently plunged into the paint pot, will lead to marks of that paint in all of the child's activity, a fallen nature will result, in varying degrees, in works of the flesh.

The Saviour Unveiled

The Fall seemed to be a victory for the Serpent, but what of the positive consequences? The reference to the "...Lamb...slain from the creation of the world" in Revelation 13:8 indicates that God in His foreknowledge had planned to work around the Serpent's activity in the Garden; hence the triumphant statements in Genesis 2:24 and 3:15.

The first of these verses could not fully apply to motherless Adam himself, but was directed to his race. More than that, it looked forward to the relationship of Christ and His Church (Ephesians 5:31-32) which would surpass even the initial bliss of Adam and Eve in their sinless state. The Second Man exercised His freewill in perfect submission to His God and Father. That unique obedience accomplished a perfect salvation and also provides for a perfect unity between Christ and

His Church. Man had a testing point for his obedience – the tree of knowledge – and he failed, but in doing so proved that he possessed true freewill, a freewill that could have been exercised in obedience to God (as was demonstrated by the Son of Man).

The final testing point for the Lord Jesus came at Calvary, where Satan attacked the Head of all creation. But the Serpent's head was bruised and Christ, as the head of a new race, gives new life and a new nature to those who become His seed. This triumph brings, and will bring, glory to God in Christ – the eternal purpose of creation:

"For in him all things were created: things in heaven and on earth, visible and invisible, whether thrones or powers or rulers or authorities; all things have been created through him and for him. He is before all things, and in him all things hold together. And he is the head of the body, the church; he is the beginning and the firstborn from among the dead, so that in everything he might have the supremacy" (Colossians 1:16-18).

Those who believe in the Lord Jesus Christ today can glorify God by surrendering their will, the right to do as they please, to His will. This logically makes them prime targets for attack by the subtle Serpent who despises the victories of the garden of Gethsemane and the Cross. We rejoice, however, that in subjection to God we can resist the Deceiver and, as James 4 tells us, he will now flee from us!

Prayer in the Battle for Souls (Guy Jarvie)

Do we wonder why we preach the Gospel and men don't immediately respond to it? It's because there are world rulers whose aim is to keep men in darkness. It is a sobering thing for us to think of how few are being turned from darkness to light through our ministry. We realize, as we think about it, how little we really know about this conflict. Our first impression - and it's a right one - is to drop upon our knees and confess before God our total inability to do anything in this in our own strength.

As we kneel before God we feel that our pride and self-sufficiency leaves us and we realize that if it wasn't for divine grace we could never wage this warfare; and if it wasn't for divine power we could never bring a soul to Christ. When we are on our knees, we are in the right place to be victors in this conflict. Until we learn to pray "with all prayer and supplication" we shall know little of victory against the spiritual hosts of wickedness.

Probably the greatest single cause of weakness among believers is the lack of prayer. Not enough time is spent in prayer and supplication. To pray alone is probably the hardest of all spiritual exercises and yet without this we cannot hope to be victorious in this conflict. God will never grant power where there is little prayer. We know that to attempt anything without divine power is to invite defeat.

We must have times of prayer alone if we are to succeed as the Lord's warriors. We must also know the Spirit's power in the prayer meetings if we are to succeed as God's people. Praise God! This power is ours if we seek it humbly with all our hearts.

16 THE BATTLE IN OUR HYMNS – OUR BATTLE (MARTIN JONES)

Another chapter in our Anthology talks about how writers of fiction have seized on the subject of spiritual warfare for their work. That is perhaps even truer of hymn-writers, as this survey of hymns found in Psalms, Hymns and Spiritual Songs (PHSS) proves! You don't have to go looking too far to find a hymn totally, or partially, devoted to this subject in one of its various aspects.

Perhaps the most common theme is to do with the Christian's own battle, where the hymn-writers urge and encourage us in it. Rather than select some well-known hymns, some of which you will find scattered throughout this Anthology, we have focused on some of the lesser known ones and in some cases the individuals who were behind them. We hope you might discover these hymns for the first time, or rediscover them, and sing them in our meetings (don't worry – in some cases alternative tunes are suggested!).

392 - O Christian Awake! For The Strife Is At Hand (Anon)

> O Christian awake! For the strife is at hand;
> With helmet and shield, and a sword in thy hand,
> To meet the bold tempter, go, fearlessly go,
> And stand like the brave, with thy face to the foe!

Whatever thy danger, take heed and beware,
But turn not thy back, for no armour is there;
The legions of darkness if thou wouldst o'er throw,
Then stand, like the brave, with thy face to the foe!

The cause of thy Master with vigour defend,
Be watchful, be zealous and fight to the end;
Wherever he leads thee, go, valiantly, go,
And stand, like the brave, with thy face to the foe!

Press on, never doubting, thy Captain is near,
With grace to supply and with comfort to cheer,
His love, like a stream in the desert, will flow,
Then stand, like the brave, with thy face to the foe!

Those of you that know your hymns well will spot that verse 2 was omitted from PHSS, potentially because it implies that believers can overthrow the legions of darkness - the reality is that Christ achieved this at Calvary – our role is to resist, not overthrow.

The chorus to this hymn (Stand like the brave, stand like the brave, stand like the brave, with your face to the foe) is perhaps better known than the verses! The meter of this hymn is 11.11.11.11, so there are a few alternatives tunes in PHSS to try out. Perhaps the most fitting of these in terms of tempo would be St Denio (Immortal, Invisible, God Only Wise) but you would probably have to dispense with the chorus...

350 – Oft in Danger, Oft in Woe (F.S. Colquhoun)

Oft in danger, oft in woe,
Onward, Christian, onward go:
Bear the toil, maintain the strife,
Strengthened with the Bread of Life.

Let not sorrow dim your eye,
Soon shall every tear be dry;
Let not fears your course impede,
Great your strength, if great your need.

Onward Christians, onward go,
Join the war and face the foe;
Will ye flee in danger's hour?
Know ye not your Captain's power?

Let your drooping hearts be glad:
March in heavenly armour clad:
Fight, nor think the battle long,
Victory soon shall be your song.

Onward then in battle move,
More than conquerors ye shall prove;
Though opposed by many a foe,
Christian soldiers, onward go.

Hymns of glory and of praise,
Father, unto Thee we raise,
Praise unto Thine only Son,
And the Spirit, Three in One.

Again, the alert may spot that this version is slightly different from that in PHSS. The third verse is omitted from PHSS but the final verse has been added to versions seen elsewhere. It is not known why this verse was added, except potentially to redirect our focus away from ourselves and back to God – it does feel a bit incongruous though.

Interestingly, PHSS credits Mrs. F.S. Colquhoun (1809-1877) with writing the words; however others ascribe the original authorship to a Henry Kirke White (1785-1806) of Nottingham, England. There is quite a background to the hymn. It was first printed in 1812, the delay caused by the fact that the manuscript was only found in his papers after his death; but then it appears that the original was added to by a Frances Sara Fuller-Maitland Colquhoun (what a mouthful) in 1827 when she was just 14 - and then a further version appears in the revised Mitre Hymn Book of 1836. Mrs. Colquhoun, as her full name indicates, was quite well-to-do - being the fourth daughter of Ebenezer Fuller-Maitland of Stanstead Hall, and Park Place, Henley-on-Thames. Frances married John Colquhoun, son of Sir James Colquhoun, in 1834.

As for White, he was the son of a butcher and had working-class origins – but he was a gifted poet. After reading Walter Scott's Force of Truth, he underwent a conversion de-scribed metaphorically in the hymn "When Marshaled on the Nightly Plain." White enrolled at St. John's College, Cam-bridge, planning to become a minister, but he sadly fell ill and died before graduation at the age of 22. Some said he destroyed his health by over-application to his studies; he was so well-known in his day that the famous poet, Byron, wrote a lament to White in English Bards and Scottish Reviewers.

For some reason, the compilers of the PHSS hymnbook did not select the tune "University College" to accompany the words, as was usual. They opted instead for "Dent Dale", arranged and harmonized by the famous English composer R. Vaughan Williams. This choice may be one of the reasons why we rarely sing this hymn!

349 - Faint not Christian (James Harrington Evans)

Faint not, Christian! Though the road
Leading to Thy blest abode
Darksome be, and dangerous too,
Christ, thy Guide, will bring thee through.

Faint not, Christian! Though in rage
Satan doth thy soul engage;
Take thee faith's anointed shield,
Bear it to the battle-field.

Faint not, Christian! Though the world
Hath its hostile flag unfurled;
Hold the Cross of Jesus fast,
Thou shalt overcome at last.

Faint not, Christian! Though within
There's a heart so prone to sin;
Christ, thy Lord, is over all,
Trusting Him, thou wilt not fall.

Faint not, Christian! Though thy God
Smite thee with the chastening rod;
Smite He must with Father's care,
That He may His love declare.

Faint not, Christian! Christ is near;
Soon in glory He'll appear;
Then shall end thy toil and strife,
Death be swallowed up of life.

The main point of this hymn is encouraging us not to faint – a more modern way of putting it might be "don't give up!" The hymn was written by James Harrington Evans, M.A., son of the Rev. Dr. Evans, vicar of Salisbury Cathedral. He was born in 1785 and educated at Wadham College, Oxford, where he graduated in 1803. Ordained in 1808, he remained in the Church of England until 1815, when he seceded and became a Baptist minister. He died in 1849.

Once again, the traditional tune appears to be "University College", which again the compilers of PHSS rejected in favour of "Da Christus." It's pure speculation whether it's this that has caused this hymn to be very rarely sung in our assemblies! If so, this could be rectified as the meter for this hymn, and also for hymn 350, is 7.7.7.7 – which means that there are a number of more well-known alternatives to choose from. Why not try "Monkland" (Let us With a Gladsome Mind), "Nottingham" (Great the Joy When Christians Meet) or perhaps "Vienna" (Great Jehovah, Living One)?

375 - The Son of God Went Forth to War (Reginald Heber)

The Son of God goes forth to war,
A kingly crown to gain;
His blood red banner streams afar:
Who follows in his train?
Who best can drink his cup of woe,
Triumphant over pain,
Who patient bears his cross below,
Who follows in his train?

That martyr first, whose eagle eye
Could pierce beyond the grave;
Who saw his Master in the sky,
And called on him to save.
Like him, with pardon on his tongue,
In midst of mortal pain,
He prayed for them that did the wrong:
Who follows in his train?

A glorious band, the chosen few
On whom the Spirit came;
Twelve valiant saints, their hope they knew,

And mocked the cross and flame.
They met the tyrant's brandished steel,
The lion's gory mane;
They bowed their heads the death to feel:
Who follows in their train?

A noble army, men and boys,
The matron and the maid,
Around the Saviour's throne rejoice,
In robes of light arrayed.
They climbed the steep ascent of heaven,
Through peril, toil and pain;
O God, to us may grace be given,
To follow in their train.

This hymn was used in the 1975 film version of "The Man Who Would Be King", starring Sean Connery and Michael Caine which was nominated for several Academy Awards. Adapted from the Rudyard Kipling short story, the film follows two rogue ex-non-commissioned officers of the Indian Army who set off from late 19th century British India in search of adventure and end up as kings of the mythical Kafiristan.

The hymn wasn't of course written specially for the film, in fact it was written for St. Stephen's Day, a religious holiday observed by the Anglican Church (Stephen being, of course, one of the great martyrs which the song speaks of). The hymn was written by Reginald Heber who was born in 1783 in Malpas, Cheshire, England. Heber attended Brasenose College, Oxford, where he won a number of awards in English and Latin. He received a fellowship to All Souls College, and later became Rector at Hodnet, Shropshire, England. In 1823, he became, somewhat reluctantly, Bishop of Calcutta, India. Reginald Heber also wrote two other hymns in PHSS "From Greenlands Icy Mountains" and the more timeless classic "Holy, Holy, Holy." Most of his hymns were not published until after his death; he died in 1826, aged just 43, in Trichinopoly (Tiruchirappalli), Tamil Nadu, India, of a cerebral hemorrhage while bathing.

PHSS uses the tune "Ellacombe" but this hymn is usually sung to other tunes. As the meter is D.C.M (which is simply the Common Meter sung twice), there are lots of alternative tunes to select from, including, perhaps, the most well-known – "Bethlehem" which is more usually used to give thanks for our food (O God to Thee, We Raise Our Voice.) This alternative seems to have the tempo that you need to match the stirring lyrics; or you could do worse than give "Blessed Name" (We Bless and Praise Thee Gracious God) a try.

393 – Christian Seek Not Yet Repose (Charlotte Elliott)

Christian, seek not yet repose,
Hear thy gracious Saviour say;
Thou art in the midst of foes:
Watch and pray.

Principalities and powers,
Mustering their unseen array,
Wait for thy unguarded hours:
Watch and pray.

Gird thy heavenly armour on,
Wear it ever night and day;
Ambushed lies the evil one:
Watch and pray.

Hear the victors who overcame,
Still they mark each warrior's way;
All with one sweet voice exclaim,

Watch and pray.

Hear, above all, hear thy Lord,
Him thou lovest to obey;
Hide within thy heart His word:
Watch and pray.

Watch, as if on that alone
Hung the issue of the day;
Pray, that help may be sent down:
Watch and pray.

"Seek Not Yet Repose" might be translated today as "Don't Put Your Feet Up Yet." The tune used in PHSS for this hymn is Vigilate. As the meter is 7.7.7.3, there is unfortunately no alternative tune in the hymnbook so there is no option but to learn it, if you don't know it already!

This hymn was written by Charlotte Elliott (1789-1871) of Clapham, England. She wrote about 150 hymns and has been described as "perhaps...the most important...woman hymn-writer...born in the eighteenth century." Physically, she was very weak and was a total invalid for much of her life. Her hymns and poems depict the inevitability of human suffering and embrace hardship and loss as roads to heaven.

Her father was a leading member of the Clapham Saints - a group of influential like-minded Church of England social reformers who, with William Wilberforce as its centre of gravity, founded the British and Foreign Bible Society, the Church Missionary Society and Freetown in Sierra Leone (the first major British colony in Africa, whose purpose was the abolition of the slave trade, the civilisation of Africa, and the introduction of the gospel there).

The story of how Charlotte became a believer is an interesting one. Patrons and invited guests gathered and witnessed a verse recital by one of the most physically beautiful young women most had ever seen; and they say that her voice was a wonder of beauty and crystal clarity. At the conclusion, and as the gathered guests raved over her, a pastor waited patiently. Privately, he introduced himself and said, "Young lady, your talent and beauty are a thing of wonder. But, without Jesus, you are no better than the lowest prostitute out in our streets!" Reeling back with shock at these words, 33 year old Charlotte gasped, "Sir! What you said is an insult beyond belief!"

That night Charlotte was troubled, restless, and could not sleep. She knelt beside her bed and prayed. A few weeks later, she saw the Pastor and apologized, saying, "I am sorry for my rudeness. Actually I would like to come to Christ, but I don't know how to find Him." He said, "Come just as you are!" and she accepted Jesus as her Saviour that day.

Twelve years later (1834), in very weakened health, she desperately wanted to help her brother raise money for St. Mary's Hall college for daughters of poor clergymen, but she couldn't see how. One morning before dawn, remembering the Pastor's words, her mind began to fill with the words of a poem that would be published anonymously two years later. Not realizing that Charlotte had written the poem, her doctor came by one day and handed her a copy of the poem leaflet. Tears streamed down her face as she read the six verses and was told that copies of the poem were being sold and the money given to St. Mary's Hall. That poem supplied the words for what would become that great and well-loved hymn "Just as I Am, Without One Plea..."

Battle Quotes 4

"Wars on earth are but tremors felt from an earthquake light-years away. The Christian's war takes place at the very epicentre of the earthquake. It is infinitely more deadly, while the issues that hang on it make earth's most momentous questions no more than village gossip. To acknowledge Jesus as Saviour and Lord is to join an army. Whether you know it or not, you have enlisted. The only other option open to you is to become a deserter, to hide your uniform and pretend you are someone you are not." (John White)

"The spiritual warfare thus depicted is not a conflict between individuals, but a vast war between opposing armies. There is no room here for "lone rangers" pursuing their individual goals. Victory will require controlled and concerted action by God's people working together. This will demand discipline and a readiness to submit to scriptural authority." (Derek Prince)

"To avoid social contact with non-Christian people is to retire within the walls of the Church's battlements. To withdraw...is to "hide our light under a bushel" or to be the salt of the earth in those little sealed plastic packages. It is to change the militant...into the besieged – a change the devil very much wants to bring about." (John White)

17 DESPATCHES FROM THE FRONT LINE – A WIFE AND MOTHER (SANDRA DORRICOTT)

The Nightmare Begins

When I said my wedding vows – "I promise to love you with all my heart, for better, for worse, for richer, for poorer, in sickness and in health" – I had no idea of what that really meant. As a young bride I only thought of the positives and the "live happy every after"! How naive I was! And yet looking back, how could I have known? You need to experience the journey of life in order to understand that no one is free of challenges and difficulties. For me, my journey was going along pretty well for a while. Yes, there were some rough times but for the most part it was OK - until I hit forty. What is it that they say – "life begins at forty"? For me it felt like a nightmare began. However, it was also an amazing experience of the sure reality of a very "special friend."

Keith, my husband, was 44 and an Executive with the Bank of Montreal. We had 3 children: Adele (17), Jennifer (14) and Andrew (almost 8). One evening, Keith came home from work and told me he had received a call from the Doctor who was quite sure that Keith had leukemia. My life changed in the second it took him to say "leukemia."

Further tests confirmed he had Chronic Lymphocytic Leukemia (CLL).

Prognosis: start on chemotherapy by pills and he could live 5 to 15 years. For a year we told no one, not even close family or our children. I was alone with it as Keith didn't want to talk or discuss it – so it was just God and me. My dependence on Him and my prayer life changed completely.

Philippians 4:6 says: "'Do not be anxious about anything, but in every situation, by prayer and petition, with thanksgiving, present your requests to God." Is it possible to be anxious about nothing? Wow - imagine me being like that! And be thankful? Well, that was asking a bit too much! Then it goes on in verse 7 to say "and the peace of God, which transcends all understanding, will guard your hearts and your minds in Christ Jesus." Boy, did my heart and mind need guarding because Satan was attacking my mind fast and furious. I very quickly also came to realize that I could come to God through His Son during what I knew was going to be the most difficult time of my life so far. Someone once told me I had made a choice - I could bring God closer into my life or I could be angry and turn away from Him. I suppose it was a choice but I have no recollection of it being a conscious one. The thing I did not want was to become angry and bitter and pass that on to my children. What would that accomplish?

A Private Problem

A year went by and Keith's leukemia got so much worse that he had to start on quite hard chemotherapy and might only have a year to live – how did this happen without any warning? Yet this went on for four long years without us going public. It became harder as he kept getting stronger chemo, lost weight and looked absolutely dreadful.

The time had come where we had to tell the children. Andrew was the last we told as he was the youngest; talk about praying day & night – "God in heaven give us the right words to say and be with this little lad when he hears about his Dad." 2 Corinthians 12:9-10 says "...my grace is sufficient for you, for my power is made perfect in weakness...for when I am weak, then I am strong." I sure was weak and truly only God's strength got me through. We were in Florida on a family vacation; we told him the first day after we got there so we could have a good fun week with him after that. He'd been studying about blood cells in school and understood what was happening to his Dad and said "but Dad - the chemo can kill those white cells and so can God". God had been preparing him to hear this news – thank you amazing God, my "special friend."

Even with God in my life, and Him pulling me up over and over again when I felt I was ten storeys up, hanging on to the outside of a window sill with my finger-tips – I still had times when I forgot to go to God and I left Him. Satan was attacking me all the time – he knew my weaknesses and he used them. It was like I was in spiritual warfare. On the day Keith started chemotherapy, the verse on our calendar was Jeremiah 21:8 "See, I am setting before you the way of life..." This verse rang in my mind a million times over in the next number of years and I felt Satan tried to destroy it. No matter how bad things got, and they got very, very bad, God always, always brought that verse into my mind. Satan on the other hand would bring thoughts like "but the Doctor said he probably wouldn't make it until Christmas", or "but you heard what the Doctor said about this or that", or "but you know the prognosis of where he is now and it's not good".

And so on it went until I could scream - in fact many a time I did just that and told Satan to depart from me in the name of the Lord Jesus Christ. I realized a few minutes later that I had this amazing peace – the peace that passes all understanding. It was a wonderful feeling. Oh, how I wished I could hang on to it but it could be swept away in a second and I had to fight to get it back. Don't be deceived - Satan wants you and wanted me to be angry and turn totally away from God;

he didn't want God to be my special friend in any shape or form and he was continually doing all he could to destroy my relationship with God.

A life of faith and prayer doesn't really come naturally to most of us and it was no different for me. It grows from tiny seeds that we plant and nurture as we mature and experience life. I heard the saying once "smooth seas don't produce skillful sailors – it's the rough waters that train them to be skillful" and so it is with God – it was, and is, the turbulent times in my life that have molded me to be a better disciple and woman of prayer and faith. Some people have said that I was so strong and so courageous – I definitely was not – it was the more I grew closer to God and saw His faithfulness over and over again, the more and more I trusted Him; but I had to learn it the hard way by being tested.

Unfortunately, it turned out that Keith had the most aggressive form of CLL that the doctors had ever seen. Over the next four years he was in and out of hospital and on and off even stronger chemotherapy. At home he would just go from the bed to the couch; no talking, just lying there and I literally had to go over and listen to see if he was dead or alive. Our house had lost its laughter and fun. I felt like I was neglecting the children and that was very difficult for me. My "special friend" was called and leaned upon so much for my children as well. At the same time God used my children to strengthen me and keep me going. I remember telling Andrew some more "bad news" about his Dad. He was very quiet and then he turned to me and said "Mom - we are going to be okay". I wasn't sure whether he thought everything would be fine with his Dad or if his faith was strong enough to know we would get through this regardless, so I said "Andrew, you are right, God will be with us and we will be okay no matter what happens". We hugged and then went back to what we were doing. It turns out that we were right; God would be with us. But, as hard as things had been up to now, we didn't know that the worst was still yet to come.

The Only Hope

Eventually, the doctor told us that our only hope was a bone marrow transplant. Back then it wasn't a common procedure at all and very high risk. To start with, we needed someone with a very high match with Keith, which wasn't guaranteed at all. Thank you, God, that Keith's sister Hilary was a perfect match – that was no coincidence. But there were still lots of obstacles to overcome – tests, counselling and the removal of Keith's spleen (it was the size of a watermelon, packed with leukemic cells which would not be killed by any chemo) - followed by "salvage chemo" to prepare his body for the transplant – yes, the name says it all.

The week that we were to find out if the chemo had worked – he needed less than 50% leukemia in his bone marrow for them to do the Bone Marrow Transplant - was very hard for me. The hymns "God holds the key of all unknown and I am glad, if other hands should hold the key I might be sad" and "not now my child a little more rough tossing!" kept ringing in my ears. Anyone who knows me will know that I don't do well with rough tossing seas, so this wasn't a good image for me at all! I called on my "special friend" almost hourly during this week. Little did I know that he was preparing me for news that I didn't want to hear - the wretched chemo had done absolutely nothing to the cancer cells so he was no longer eligible for a transplant. Talk about feeling like your balloon just burst – in other words "take your husband home and enjoy the short time you have together. There is nothing more we can do."

Oh my! I need to tell my dear children bad news again. God in heaven give me your strength – I can't do this on my own. Many tears flowed that day; but life goes on and the days come and go whether we want them to or not. A year was just about up and Keith's counts were the worst the lab had ever encountered. The doctor decided to try another combination of chemo's – there was no alternative but to try. Our home became a hospital again. How much more can I take of this? By this point I had been having pain in my chest and arm, not sleeping, not involved with anybody else – this had become my whole life and I was absolutely wiped out. My kids were suffering; Keith was at the end of himself. God what is happening? Where are you taking us? I am not kidding that if my "special friend" wasn't in my life I would have ended up in a mental hospital. The toll over nine years was almost more than my body and mind could take - there were times when I would get home from the hospital and think "how did I get here?" I couldn't even remember driving home. Thank you, God, for my "guardian angel" - who I think did double time during these years.

Crisis Point

Unfortunately, this chemo caused fluid to build up in Keith's lung cavity and he had to be re-admitted to hospital. They drained off the fluid day after day, as it kept building continually. The doctor decided Keith needed surgery to remove as much fluid as possible and see if they could find out what was going on. He would then need to be admitted to Intensive Care. A bed was supposed to coming up within a few hours but there was no guarantee one would be available in time. Keith was hooked up to oxygen with the full mask and tubes everywhere. He still had trouble breathing and looked like every breath was his last. I had planned his funeral out before but now in my mind I was finalizing the details. My heart was breaking – I was in tears. I was pleading with the Doctor to find Keith a spot in the unit and with my "special friend" to just help all of us because I really didn't know what to pray for. Keith had told me a few hours before that he had enough of this fighting and couldn't do it any more – did he need my permission to let go? Could I do that for him? It sounds easy but it was one of the hardest moments through this experience. How could he just die on us and not fight? I had fought for him for nine years - why couldn't he keep on fighting?

Of course I knew the answers – I felt the same way, but rationale goes out the window at a time like this and you are faced with the moment.

The fluid continued to come back. I just felt this really is it. I need to call my brother and ask him to go to visit a funeral home with me. This just made me sick to my stomach – was this really going to be the end? Nine years of fighting for his life, of giving up my life to do everything for him and for my family – I didn't even know who I was anymore. I was angry, sad, mad, scared and relieved all rolled into one. Did I need my "special friend"? Where was He? Why couldn't I find Him? I realized I had to take a deep breath to calm myself and to start praying even although, at this point, I really didn't feel like it. Gradually I felt God's presence again and His peace coming into my heart and mind. I'd found my way back to my "special friend" and knew that as long as I kept close to Him I would get through whatever was ahead.

To cut a long story short, God opened up a bed in Intensive Care and Keith survived. Miraculously (that's how the doctors described it), the fluid stopped collecting one day and didn't come back. They didn't know how or why – but I knew that the prayers to my "special friend" had been heard and answered. I was so relieved and yet the journey was still ongoing – what next? A big surprise! Against all expectations, the doctor said "you're probably able to have your transplant now. But there is a very small window of opportunity for you to take." Wow - it was a very scary time for me. Keith was feeling relatively well and to have him go into another life and death experience after what we had just gone through was almost too much to bear. What a hard decision to make and yet there was really no decision to make – he was running out of borrowed time. Leaving the house on the day of the transplant, I felt like my insides were being ripped out of me; seeing Andrew & Jennifer have to say good-bye – was their Dad coming home? Only God knew the answer to that question. When Keith was admitted, the doctor again went over all the pros and cons – there were more cons than pros. I just thought to myself "why on earth are we doing this?" - but there we were. We were both in God's hands and I had to trust my "special friend" to get me through no matter what.

Chemo like Keith had never had before started and his hair fell out for the third time - it never got any easier to see. His immune system was zero so he was in a special filtered room for the whole time. I can't tell you how many bowls of sickness I held, measured and cleaned up for my dear husband – it was not a pretty picture. This went on for weeks. Keith was so ill he couldn't talk, wanted me there all the time and sometimes I wasn't the best company for him. There were times when I just felt like throwing that horrible bowl of sickness across the room and saying "No more, I can't do it!" (Fortunately common sense took over and I didn't – I'd just have more mess to clean up.) My migraines were so severe sometimes and I was so drugged that I lay down on his floor with an ice pack on my head. I couldn't miss a day – Keith needed me. But guess what? God strengthened me in those times and I did keep going – this still amazes me today when I think of it. Amazing grace!

The End in Sight?

There were many tough days and times when we, and the doctors, wondered if he might be rejecting the transplant. But after six weeks Keith got home from hospital. He couldn't go out for 100 days and was in and out of hospital quite a bit in this time with infections. It seemed over - but was it? When a year was up they did tests to see what was left of the leukemia in his marrow. His chance of the leukemia not returning was only 25% - not good odds. But I had a big God, my "special friend" who had brought me this far. I can honestly say that I thought He would bring me and Keith all the way – but of course Satan was as active as ever. The nurse called with the results and I answered the phone with my heart beating a mile a minute. This was it – no turning back. "There is no evidence of any leukemia cells at all in Keith's bone marrow." I repeated it to her and she said "Sandra, this is great news!" I replied, "I know! But can you please repeat it so I know I'm hearing you correctly?" So she did! Could this eleven year battle really be over? My mind couldn't really comprehend this all at once. For eleven years this was my whole life and now – he really had no leukemia? God has answered so many prayers all these years. Why had it taken him so long? Only God knows that but praise God he did. It was, and is, truly a miracle.

Life throws us many different challenges and God, my "special friend" was with me all the way. My prayer life and my trust in Him became so much deeper as a result. It changed my relationship with Him for the rest of my life. Would I want to go through it again? I have to say I'd rather not - but I am not sorry that I have such a relationship with my God and Saviour that I may never have had if this ordeal hadn't happened to me and my family. Just over a year ago my husband was diagnosed with Parkinson's – it doesn't seem fair does it? Who said life is fair? He is alive and well almost 14 years after his transplant – is that fair? That is wonderful – this isn't always the case. So my journey of life continues and who knows what lies ahead? Personally, I'd rather not know. Whatever it is, my "special friend" will see me through.

A Call to Arms (John Drain)

In recent years many brothers and sisters among God's people have put off their armour, and put it off forever. They have been taken to the rest of heaven from the arena of conflict. There are others who are not as able as they once were for front line action. Are there young men and women who are realizing the increasing need to put on the armour for the holy warfare of the Faith of our Lord Jesus Christ?

We are often impressed by the sacrifice which young people are willing to make in loyalty to the cause of their nation. What about God's holy nation? Never was there a time when young brothers and sisters were more needed to shoulder the claims and support the cause of that nation. In a military operation it is a mistake to underestimate the power of the enemy, and it is a serious defect to lack intelligence covering the strategy and tactics of the attacking force.

The strike power of the enemy forces is staggering. We daren't think for one moment that in our own strength we can resist or overcome the opposition. What should we do? Give up in despair? The answer to this must be, No! God has told us plainly what to do:

"Put on the full armour of God, so that you can take your stand against the devil's schemes...Therefore put on the full armour of God, so that when the day of evil comes, you may be able to stand your ground, and after you have done everything, to stand" (Ephesians 6:11, 13).

18 ISRAEL'S BATTLE - NEHEMIAH (REG DARKE)

"...We will not neglect the house of our God." (Nehemiah 10)

When Nehemiah came to Jerusalem and found the walls of the city broken down and the gates burned with fire, and only a few of God's people left, he might well have thrown up his hands in despair and left the work for someone else to do. But he didn't. Strengthened by prayer and a godly determination to labour for the Lord, Nehemiah not only revived the spirits of an apparently defeated people by words of encouragement, but inspired them to rise up and build for God. This is what men of God are expected to do. How easy it is to give up, resign, and leave the work for someone else; to be like Ephraim and turn back in the day of battle, or like Demas, who left Paul in the lurch because fields further away appeared greener!

The bold, determined pledge not to forsake the house of God was made by a man who had known more than his share of adversity, criticism, and personal attacks, but he stood like a rock through it all. Nehemiah means "the consolation of Jehovah", and this is what he proved to be when God's people had their backs to the wall. Laughed to scorn, maligned, ridiculed, despised, and reproached, Nehemiah could easily have resigned and returned to the quiet isolation of Shushan; but instead he took up the challenge to be a restorer of God's people and house, and he revealed himself to be God's man in time of crisis.

Today the Lord is looking for men and women who are not easily discouraged when the tide runs strongly against them. We must realize, as Paul did, that the house of God is the adversary's main target. He knows that he cannot triumph over the Body of Christ, for the Lord has decreed that "...the gates of Hades will not overcome it". But he can succeed against the churches of God, and his attempts to do so will not cease until the Lord comes. We must not be ignorant of his devices; we must not encourage his work through our own folly, our unwise actions and attitudes, our unkind words, our lack of zeal, or tendency to depression or discouragement.

We must, as in Nehemiah's day, work together with trowel and sword on the wall, or below the wall clearing away the rubble. Criticisms will be made of us because we are few in number, and some will also say that it is presumption for such a weak people to claim to be the house of God. But Nehemiah experienced the same thing:

"What are those feeble Jews doing? Will they restore their wall? Will they offer sacrifices? Will they finish in a day? Can they bring the stones back to life from those heaps of rubble - burned as they are...? What they are building - even a fox climbing up on it would break down their wall of stones!" (Nehemiah 4:2-3).

Did Nehemiah walk away from the work because of such criticism? No, he committed the whole matter to the Lord in prayer, and got on with the job.

"Hear us our God for we are despised ... so we rebuilt the wall ... for the people worked with all their heart" (Nehemiah 4:4, 6).

Conspiracies and threats of war followed, but Nehemiah prayed, worked on and watched on. So the work proceeded and they built the wall and restored the gates, labouring by day and guarding by night. It was a full-time job. What dedication! What a love for God and His house! No sacrifice was too great, and no wonder the claim was triumphantly made, "Our God shall fight for us."

Surely we can see here a lesson that we have to learn today, that the house is the Lord's, the battle is the Lord's, and the ability to prosper is the Lord's! The arm of flesh must fail; humans fail, and so will humanly inspired programmes; but God never fails, and neither does His love. We did not put ourselves into the Fellowship of His Son, we were called by God into it (see 1 Corinthians 1:9), and God does not call us out to join some other movement. We go out of our own accord, or we are put out for a scriptural reason. It is God's intention that those called should remain in His house from the moment they are built in as living stones (see 1 Peter 2:5). Our constant prayer should be: "One thing I ask from the LORD, this only do I seek: that I may dwell in the house of the LORD all the days of my life, to gaze on the beauty of the LORD and to seek him in his temple" (Psalm 27:4).

Those who pledged themselves with Nehemiah not to forsake the house of God brought for the divine dwelling-place a "heave offering" - a present of corn, wine and oil. Might this indicate to us today that if we have a true appreciation of the Lord Jesus as our food (corn) and joy (wine), and the power of the indwelling Holy Spirit (oil), we will be contented, happy, Spirit-led Christians, eager to work in God's house, and with absolutely no thought of forsaking it?

May God give us the strength and courage to stand and not be easily moved. During one crisis Nehemiah stood up and said to the nobles, the officials and the rest of the people: "...Don't be afraid of them. Remember the Lord, who is great and awesome, and fight for your families, your sons and your daughters, your wives and your homes" (Nehemiah 4:14). Let this be also true of us.

Battle Bible Verses 1

Matthew 6:20-21: "But store up for yourselves treasures in heaven, where moths and vermin do not destroy and where thieves do not break in and steal. For where your treasure is, there your heart will be also."

Romans 6:16-18: "Don't you know that when you offer yourselves to someone as obedient slaves, you are slaves of the one you obey - whether you are slaves to sin, which leads to death, or to obedience, which leads to righteousness? But thanks be to God that, though you used to be slaves to sin, you have come to obey from your heart the pattern of teaching that has now claimed your allegiance. You have been set free from sin and have become slaves to righteousness."

Ephesians 3:16-19: "I pray that out of his glorious riches he may strengthen you with power through his Spirit in your inner being, so that Christ may dwell in your hearts through faith. And I pray that you, being rooted and established in love, may have power, together with all the Lord's holy people, to grasp how wide and long and high and deep is the love of Christ, and to know this love that surpasses knowledge - that you may be filled to the measure of all the fullness of God."

19 PAUL'S BATTLE – THE THORN IN THE FLESH (MARTIN JONES)

"I know a man in Christ who fourteen years ago was caught up to the third heaven. Whether it was in the body or out of the body I do not know - God knows. And I know that this man - whether in the body or apart from the body I do not know, but God knows - was caught up to paradise and heard inexpressible things, things that no one is permitted to tell.

I will boast about a man like that, but I will not boast about myself, except about my weaknesses. Even if I should choose to boast, I would not be a fool, because I would be speaking the truth. But I refrain, so no one will think more of me than is warranted by what I do or say, or because of these surpassingly great revelations. Therefore, in order to keep me from becoming conceited, I was given a thorn in my flesh, a messenger of Satan, to torment me. Three times I pleaded with the Lord to take it away from me.

But he said to me, 'My grace is sufficient for you, for my power is made perfect in weakness.' Therefore I will boast all the more gladly about my weaknesses, so that Christ's power may rest on me. That is why, for Christ's sake, I delight in weaknesses, in insults, in hardships, in persecutions, in difficulties. For when I am weak, then I am strong" (2 Corinthians 12:2-10).

The apostle Paul may, at times, have looked like a duck bobbing serenely on the surface of life - but underneath his spiritual feet were paddling furiously in a battle just to keep afloat. It can be hard, especially for Christian leaders, to admit that not everything is plain sailing in their Christian experience – in part because no-one wants to let the side down. But countless Christians have been really helped by Paul's slightly cryptic account of his thorn in the flesh – taking a lot of encouragement from the fact that Paul found himself in a very tough battle, and also from his victory strategy.

We'll come back to the strategy at the end, but first of all we'll try and address the question of exactly what this thorn in the flesh might have been. C.H. Spurgeon said (rather tongue-in-cheek perhaps) that in his experience, most people tended to explain what it was by reference to their own personal afflictions! Certainly, a very wide range of proposals have been made and we are going to cover some of them here.

Option 1 – Eyesight

Perhaps one of the most commonly seen explanations is that Paul was suffering from poor vision. Some have gone further and attributed the defect to the dazzling light which shone around him at his conversion. This view would appear to be supported by a number of verses: "As you know, it was because of an illness that I first preached the gospel to you, and even though my illness was a trial to you, you did not treat me with contempt or scorn..." (Galatians 4:13-14).

This verse indicates that the "thorn" was visible or at least noticeable to the churches that he visited, although it is hard to see how poor sight would have been a trial to them, nor is it clear why this would be the cause of preaching. "...I can testify that, if you could have done so, you would have torn out your eyes and given them to me" (Galatians 4:15).

The appearance of this verse so closely after verse 14 does seem quite compelling. Why would the Galatians feel the need to give their eyes to Paul, unless he needed them? Of course, there is no guarantee that Paul had poor sight in his mind as being a thorn, even if he did have a sight defect.

"For some say, 'His letters are weighty and forceful, but in person he is unimpressive and his speaking amounts to nothing'" (2 Corinthians 10:10).

It is suggested that one of the reasons why Paul was unimpressive in person was because of his poor vision. This is a supposition and there could be other factors at play, including the sound of his voice and his size. "Paul replied, 'Brothers, I did not realize that he was the high priest; for it is written: "Do not speak evil about the ruler of your people'" (Acts 23:5). This is certainly an intriguing verse. We must accept that Paul was speaking the truth when he said that he did not recognize the High Priest (he wasn't being ironic!) – but how could this have happened? The High Priest would probably have been wearing distinctive clothing and he would also have been a very well-known person. One explanation is that Paul was so short-sighted that he could not distinguish one member of the Sanhedrin from the other.

"I, Tertius, who wrote down this letter, greet you in the Lord" (Romans 16:22).

Some have said that Paul only used a scribe because his eyesight was so poor. This is linked to the next verse where Paul is not using a scribe: "See what large letters I use as I write to you with my own hand!" (Galatians 6:11).

Option 2 - Fits

Others have supposed that the "thorn in the flesh" refers to continual fits. Borg and Crossan speculate - and they make it clear that this is conjecture - that Paul may have been afflicted by bouts of malaria. They point out that Tarsus, Paul's hometown, had an environment that was conducive to the spread of malaria:

"Think for a moment...about that Cilician plain locked between the mountains and the sea. Think of its rich fertility and agricultural prosperity fed by three rivers that annually drained the melting snows of the Taurus range. Despite the best Roman drainage engineering, that environment also meant marshes, mosquitoes, and malaria." (The First Paul, p. 62)

They propose that Paul may have suffered from chronic malaria fever, which would be associated with, in the words of Pauline scholar William Mitchell Ramsay, "very distressing and prostrating paroxysm where the sufferer can only lie and feel himself a shaking and helpless weakling." If this is what Paul was experiencing when he was among the Galatians, we can see how it might have put a strain on them. However, it is still not clear why this would have been the cause of his preaching. There does not appear to be any scriptural evidence that Paul suffered from either epilepsy or malaria.

Option 3 – Temper

Another view which has been maintained is that this "thorn" was simply bad temper, to which Paul occasionally gave in to. The sharp disagreement of Acts 15:39 and the apparent rudeness of Acts 23:2 are given as two examples. Paul also famously tore a strip off Peter when he thought Peter was guilty of hypocrisy and some of the discourse in 2 Corinthians could be viewed as being quite angry.

There is no doubt that Paul often spoke very frankly. The subject of "boldness of speech" was a very live topic in those days – the Cynic philosophers were famous for being very blunt, to the point of rudeness and it was actually seen as a virtue by them. They saw it as being preferable to being scheming and under-handed. Did he ever cross the line and lose his temper unrighteously? Quite possibly, for Paul was human like everyone else! Was it a big enough problem to be described as a messenger from Satan though? And how does this relate to his preaching to the Galatians?

Option 4 - Homosexuality

A very controversial theory has been proposed by the ultra-liberal Episcopalian Bishop John Shelby Spong (in his book Rescuing the Bible from Fundamentalism) which suggests that it refers to homosexual tendencies. Space precludes a full review of this proposal but it is based largely on speculation and an absence of concrete evidence. Apart from alleging that Paul was a woman-hater (based on his teaching on the role of women), Spong is convinced that Paul suffered greatly from sexual temptation and passion. Although he does not support this by scriptural references, one possible allusion is 2 Corinthians 11:29 – however this could refer to any manner of sins or temptations, sexual and non-sexual. Spong concludes that, given Paul did not take his own advice to marry to deal with lust, Paul must therefore have been homosexual. Spong also points out that, given the view of homosexuality in the ancient world, this fact would have been hard for the Churches to deal with, as allegedly hinted at Galatians 4 – however this assumes that Paul's sexuality was obvious and also does not explain why his sexuality should be cause for preaching of the gospel.

There is no doubt that Paul strongly and clearly condemned acting on such desires in his other writings – see Romans 1:26-27, 1 Corinthians 6:9, and 1 Timothy 1:10. This does not rule out the possibility that Paul was a celibate homosexual (and therefore would not be sinning) and even Spong does not try to assert that Paul was actively engaged in homosexual behaviour. It is certainly possible to see how such a state of affairs could have been seen as a real "thorn in the flesh" for Paul - as it is today for some Christians - but, like all of the theories advanced, there is no unequivocal evidence to support it, nor is it an argument to support homosexuality as Spong purports.

Option 5 – Persecutions and Trials

"...I have worked much harder, been in prison more frequently, been flogged more severely, and been exposed to death again and again. Five times I received from the Jews the forty lashes minus one. Three times I was beaten with rods, once I was pelted with stones, three times I was shipwrecked, I spent a night and a day in the open sea, I have been constantly on the move.

I have been in danger from rivers, in danger from bandits, in danger from my fellow Jews, in danger from Gentiles; in danger in the city, in danger in the country, in danger at sea; and in danger from false believers. I have laboured and toiled and have often gone without sleep; I have known hunger and thirst and have often gone without food; I have been cold and naked. Besides everything else, I face daily the pressure of my concern for all the churches. Who is weak, and I do not feel weak?..." (2 Corinthians 11:23-29).

The previous four options laid out above have all dealt with things that were internal to Paul, either physically or mentally. Option 5 takes a different approach and focuses on the fact that the weaknesses referred to in the passage do not necessarily refer to illness or sickness, or in fact anything personal to Paul at all. 2 Corinthians 11:29 speaks of Paul's weakness in the context of a real laundry list of external events and impositions on Paul – which are a mixture of natural disaster, deliberate persecution and deprivation of the basics of life (food, water, clothing and safety). When you think of all that Paul endured, you would be able to forgive any of Paul's companions who decided that they didn't want to board the next ship with him – disaster of some sort was likely to strike!

In Acts 14:19, Paul was stoned and left for dead, but God raised him up and, remarkably, the next day he walked at least twenty miles into the next town and started preaching again. Can you imagine what those that stoned him must have thought? They could see Paul's humanity in the cuts and bruises, but they could also see the supernatural strength of God flowing through him; and so Paul could say: "For when I am weak, then am I strong."

This option would seem to have a good link with the previously discussed passage in Galatians. The major cities of Galatia were Derbe, Lystra, and Iconium. The instance we mentioned earlier, where Paul was stoned and left for dead, happened in Lystra and the next town was Derbe. He must have looked a real mess when he preached to them for the first time – they may have asked him, "Paul, why do you look like that?" and that could have given him the opportunity to preach the gospel. The major drawback to this option is that the thorn in the flesh does sound like something that was very personal to Paul – and not an external trial; but there can be no doubt that physical suffering was a huge part of Paul's battle.

Option 6 – The "Super-Apostles"

Some commentators have looked back to the Old Testament for clues as to what a Jewish person would mean by using the phrase "the thorn in the flesh". Here are three occasions where it occurs:

"No longer will the people of Israel have malicious neighbours who are painful briers and sharp thorns. Then they will know that I am the Sovereign LORD" (Ezekiel 28:24).

"then you may be sure that the LORD your God will no longer drive out these nations before you. Instead they will become snares and traps for you, whips on your backs and thorns in your eyes, until you perish from this good land which the LORD your God has given you." (Joshua 23:13).

"Therefore I also said, 'I will not drive them out before you; but they shall be thorns in your side, and their gods shall be a snare to you'" (Judges 2:3 NKJV).

The argument is made that each of these references relates to a group of people. What group of people could Paul have been referring to, perhaps? Is there a clue in what Paul talks a lot about in the previous chapter?

"For such people are false apostles, deceitful workers, masquerading as apostles of Christ. And no wonder, for Satan himself masquerades as an angel of light. It is not surprising, then, if his servants also masquerade as servants of righteousness..." (2 Corinthians 11:13-15).

God's Apostles are "sent ones" by God – false apostles are sent by Satan – in effect, they are his messengers who do his bidding. Is Paul talking about how he has suffered at their hands in 2 Corinthians 12:10; things such as slander, innuendo, misrepresentation, and defamation? Then, right after Paul talks about his thorn in the flesh, he brings up the false apostles again saying:

"I have made a fool of myself, but you drove me to it. I ought to have been commended by you, for I am not in the least inferior to the 'super-apostles', even though I am nothing" (2 Corinthians 12:11).

It seems that in most places that Paul planted a church, a group of detractors opposed his ministry and sought to discredit his apostolic authority in the eyes of the Christians for which he cared, as well as unsettling and confusing the Christians themselves; just look again at Galatia as an example:

"...some people are throwing you into confusion and are trying to pervert the gospel of Christ" (Galatians 1:7).

"As for those agitators, I wish they would go the whole way and emasculate themselves!" (Galatians 5:12).

"...The one who is throwing you into confusion, whoever that may be, will have to pay the penalty" (Galatians 5:10).

Are the people being referred to here the super-apostles of 2 Corinthians? You can almost hear a prayer behind the following statement in which Paul is asking the Lord to remove this person who is troubling him and the churches: "From now on, let no one cause me trouble, for I bear on my body the marks of Jesus" (Galatians 6:17).

These marks on the body could potentially be an intriguing reference to the thorn in the flesh. One day, when we get to heaven, we might be queuing up to find out from Paul exactly what he was talking about!

The Point of the Thorn

Perhaps Paul, ironically, was deliberately vague about what this thorn was because he didn't want us to concentrate on that, but on the strategy that he employed in the battle against it! This strategy is guaranteed to work for us against all thorns in the flesh and all of the circumstances that life throws at us – but that does not mean that it is an easy strategy to execute.

•"When I am weak, then I am strong" – this is brilliantly counter-intuitive and takes some of us a life-time to get our head around. When we are weak, our ego doesn't get in the way and we can be confident that when we try to do something, even in our weakness, that we are doing it for the right motives and not for our own glory. It is good to practice this by sometimes stepping outside our comfort zone and doing something different, relying on God to make up for our own pitiful shortcomings. Think of something you might not like to do in terms of God's things – and have a go!

•"My grace is sufficient for you" – if only we could rely on this great promise from the Lord Himself. Jesus' grace was sufficient enough for Him to say "Not my will, but yours be done" in the garden. It was sufficient enough for Him to say "Father, forgive them, for they do not know what they are doing" when He had been nailed to the cross. It was sufficient to say "Feed my lambs" to the one who had let Him down so badly just a few days earlier. It is more than sufficient for us – it is limitless. May we learn to trust in the sufficiency of this grace.

•"…that Christ's power may rest on me" – Paul was willing to undergo great trials if it meant that he got to experience Christ's power in a way that he wouldn't have done otherwise – the power that created the universe and keeps it going, the power that defeated Satan at the Cross, the power that will ultimately transform us miserable creatures into being "like Him." The woman who only touched the hem of His garment knew that was all she needed in the trial she had experienced for so long – just to be near Him and have His power rest on her. May we know just a tiny part of that infinite power in our individual and collective battles.

•"for Christ's sake" – ultimately for Paul, this was what life was all about – for Christ. The world uses that phrase as nothing more than a meaningless expletive these days, but it means so much more than that to us – or it should. Why do we put up with whatever each of us is putting up with in the battle – disappointment, betrayal, depression, trials, inexplicable events, temptation, sacrifices, fallings-out, rejection, misunderstanding, unpopularity, persecution (just to name a few) – isn't it all for Christ's sake? If we can view life through that lens, it is bound to change our whole perspective.

Who is on the Lord's Side?

Who is on the Lord's side? Who will serve the King?
Who will be His helpers, other lives to bring?
Who will leave the world's side? Who will face the foe?
Who is on the Lord's side? Who for Him will go?
By Thy great redemption, by Thy grace divine,
We are on the Lord's side - Saviour, we are Thine!

Not for weight of glory, nor for crown and palm,
Enter we the army, raise the warrior psalm;
But for love that claimeth lives for whom He died:
He whom Jesus nameth must be on His side.
By Thy love constraining, by Thy grace divine,
We are on the Lord's side - Saviour, we are Thine!

Jesus, Thou hast bought us, not with gold or gem,
But with Thine own life blood, for Thy diadem;
With Thy blessing filling each who comes to Thee,
Thou hast made us willing, Thou hast made us free.
By Thy great redemption, by Thy grace divine,
We are on the Lord's side - Saviour, we are Thine!

Fierce may be the conflict, strong may be the foe,
But the King's own army none can overthrow;
'Round His standard ranging, victory is secure,
For His truth unchanging makes the triumph sure.

Joyfully enlisting, by Thy grace divine,
We are on the Lord's side - Saviour, we are Thine!

Chosen to be soldiers, in an alien land,
Chosen, called, and faithful, for our Captain's band,
In the service royal, let us not grow cold;
Let us be right loyal, noble, true and bold.
Master, Thou wilt keep us, by Thy grace divine,
Always on the Lord's side - Saviour, always Thine!
Francis Ridley Havergal

20 THE HIDDEN BATTLE – ANGELS (IAN LITHGOW)

How many angels were created?

Revelation 5:11 reads: "Then I looked and heard the voice of many angels, numbering thousands upon thousands, and ten thousand times ten thousand. They encircled the throne and the living creatures and the elders."

There are also angels who sinned and who are reserved for judgement (see 2 Peter 2:4; Jude 6). In Revelation 12:7, we read of a future war between Michael and the dragon and his angels. We therefore conclude that there are incalculable numbers of angels. Ezekiel 28:13–15 gives us information about how angels were brought into being, revealing the great difference between these created beings and the human race. Angels are created perfect and have no maturing process, whereas every human passes through various stages before becoming an adult.

What is their purpose?

In the Old Testament in particular it did not seem to be something out of the ordinary that men and women knew angelic ministry. Our experience is different as we, in all probability, have never seen an angel, nor are we conscious of angelic assistance in the same way as those in former days. Could it be that in this day of grace angelic activity is not as necessary owing to the indwelling of the Holy Spirit in the believer? Note the scripture in 2 Thessalonians 2:7: "For the secret power of lawlessness is already at work; but the one who now holds it back will continue to do so till he is taken out of the way."

If we take the view that 'he' in this verse is referring to the Holy Spirit, then His restraining power will be withdrawn after the rapture of the Church, which could be a reason why angelic activity is prominent throughout the book of Revelation. Nevertheless, it is clearly stated in Hebrews 1:14 that they are all "...ministering spirits sent to serve those who will inherit salvation."

Is there a hierarchy within their ranks?

All angelic creation seem to appear in the male gender (see examples in Genesis 19:1-2; Mark 16:5; Luke 1:19); equally they neither marry nor experience death (see Luke 20:35, 36). The description of the angel Michael as "one of the chief princes" (Daniel 10:13), and as "the great prince" (Daniel 12:1), coupled with Jude's clear delineation of him as "Michael the archangel" (see also Revelation 12:7), clearly indicates position. The same inference can be drawn from the way in which the angel Gabriel is referred to in Daniel 8:16 and 9:21 as well as his statement "...I am Gabriel. I stand in the presence of God..." (Luke 1:19).

Within their ranks there is also diversity of shape and form: we read of angels in the form of men and creatures with wings and other differences in their anatomy. Was the form of angelic creation found in Genesis 3:24 where God placed cherubim at the east of the garden of Eden superior in rank to other angels? It would appear that there are a limited number of cherubim among the vast hosts of angels (see also Ezekiel 10).

Isaiah chapter 6 is the only place in Scripture where seraphim are mentioned. There, they are also spoken of in the plural, but without the definite article, which perhaps suggests that although they are numerous, they are possibly higher in rank, given their close association with the presence and glory of the Lord. Their form also appears distinct from that which we generally associate with angels. Various references to angelic beings are found in Ephesians 1:21, 3:10 and Colossians 1:16. These scriptures clearly indicate responsibility, organisation and order within the ranks of angels.

Do angels have personal names?

Yes, but only two angels out of the countless multitudes are named in Scripture: Gabriel and Michael. Their names reveal a close proximity to God. The nature of Michael's service is particularly towards the nation of Israel and to specific individuals within Israel. Revelation 1:1 and 22:16 both use the personal pronoun when speaking about the angel in question - perhaps indicating a sphere of service uniquely and singularly discharged on behalf of the Son of God?

Taking the Strongholds (Alan Toms)

1 Chronicles 11 records David's third and final anointing as king. All Israel gathered themselves together and pledged their allegiance to him. David was king over the whole land except for the stronghold of Zion where the proud Jebusites still held their ground. Their presence was a challenge to David's sovereignty and that could never be tolerated. He offered to make chief and captain the first of his men to smash the Jebusites and the honour went to Joab. Scripture (NKJV) simply says "David took the stronghold of Zion." It offered no resistance to him. "And David became more and more powerful, because the Lord Almighty was with him." Many years before, in the vale of Elah, he had proved the power of the name of the Lord of hosts and years later he was still gaining victories through that name. "And David dwelt in the stronghold; therefore they called it the city of David" (NKJV). It was his city because he conquered it.

Strongholds are still being conquered, as the victory is claimed by faith in God. "The weapons we fight with...have divine power to demolish strongholds" (2 Corinthians 10:4). Satan loves to exalt high things against the knowledge of God and he will do so in our lives if he is allowed to. Some sins get so strong a hold in a Christian's life it seems they will never be driven out. But the scripture plainly says "...sin shall no longer be your master..." (Romans 6:14). Complete victory over sin is part of our spiritual inheritance and that in every area of our lives. There is no reason why the enemy should gain the advantage.

Every sin tolerated in our hearts is a challenge to the sovereignty of our Master. Is He not Lord and King? Have we not invited Him to be so? Then let us claim His promises by faith, and do away with secret sins. The life that we now live, let us live it in faith, the faith which is in the Son of God who loved us and gave Himself up for us.

21 THE BATTLE FOR...THE HEART, MIND AND STRENGTH (MARTIN JONES)

Heart Target – Submission

The battle for the soul, once won, is won for ever and Satan is forced to settle for a second prize. His next focus of attack is to rob God of his rightful place as number one in our hearts. This is an ongoing battle. The very word submission is a dirty word even amongst some Christians, but it is at the very root of God's plan.

The Heart - Enemy Strategy

Here are three ways that Satan will try to subvert our submission so that in effect we are submitting to him and not to God:

•Independence – ever since the Garden of Eden man has had a desire to be independent and master of his own destiny. This trait seems to be ever more a threat in modern society with its focus on human rights, individual expression and belief in relativism rather than absolute truth. Satan can exploit this very skillfully.

•Investing wrongly – Jesus said that where our treasure is, there will our heart be also. He encourages us to lay up our treasures in heaven where there is permanent value. Satan dangles all sorts of carrots in front of us that cause us to invest our time, money, efforts and desires into things which may or may not be wrong in themselves but distract us from what (or who) should be our number one focus in life.

•Issues of Life – every one of us at some point in our lives comes up against events or circumstances that we would rather not have to experience. This inevitability doesn't seem to stop them from knocking us off our stride and may cause us to blame God, doubt His involvement and care for us in our lives, or at the very least cause practical hindrances and barriers. Whilst Satan may not be the instigator of each circumstance (as sometimes things are sent by God to test and prove us) he certainly is motivated to ensure that the outcome is negative.

The Heart - Defence Mechanism

•Effective priority setting – time management is a critical component of success in business and in life, but the root of it is one level up in deciding what is or is not important in life. We spend much more time thinking about how we invest our money wisely than we do about how we invest our time. And yet, it is how we invest our time that will be much more important in the final analysis of our lives. Time management tools can help, but they can only build on a big picture decision to put God first.

•Exercising faith muscles – "stepping out in faith" is a well-used term amongst Christians, although it is very hard to do in practice. It requires us to give up control of what we do, in both the small things and big things in life. Proverbs 3:5-6 sums it up: "Trust in the LORD with all your heart and lean not on your own understanding; in all your ways submit to him, and he will make your paths straight."

•Accountability to/support from fellow Christians – God knows that humans need each other to function in most activities. God identified right from the beginning that it was not good for man to be alone. This applies to keeping our hearts in the right place before God. "Keeping each other honest" in an open, constructive and non-judgemental way is a critical skill to master no matter on which side of the relationship we happen to be on any given day.

•Praise – praising God, in writing, by physical expression, in our minds or in song is helpful to take the focus away from ourselves and put the focus on God, who He is and what He has done.

•Prayer and Meditation – "Satan trembles when he sees the weakest saint upon their knees." Prayer can deteriorate to become a shopping list for the things we want or need or a reflex response in times of trouble. It needs to be a daily practice which has a much broader perspective and flows into a thoughtful consideration of God and His things.

The Mind Target – Sanctification

From Paul's writing it seems clear that the battle for his heart wasn't the biggest issue for him – it was the battle for his mind. He knew what he wanted to do, but he wasn't able to do it – and the things he didn't want to do, he ended up doing! Although he asked to be rescued from this "body of death" and although we tend to think of our flesh being the big problem, the fact is that everything starts with our minds – our mind controls what we end up doing, saying and seeing.

If Satan loses the battle for your heart, the next prize will be to nullify your best intentions by playing a series of mind games. God wants your mind to be sanctified – to be set apart, to be clear-headed, pure and holy. Satan wants to mess with it so that it is polluted and muddled.

The Mind - Enemy Strategy

·Conformity – as JB Phillips put it, Satan wants to squeeze us into the world's mould, so that we think just like everyone else and take a worldview which is very different from God's.

·Confusion – there are so many brands of non-Christian teaching, Christian teaching and quasi-Christian teaching that it can be difficult to know what you should believe and practise.

·Cacophony – we live in an information age where our senses are constantly bombarded with a vast amount of images and information which carry a risk of what is of truly lasting importance and value being drowned out.

The Mind - Defence Mechanism

· Bringing every thought into the obedience of Christ
· Renewing of the mind
· Putting on the Mind of Christ
· Using the Sword of the Spirit
· Holding onto the pattern of sound teaching
· Whatever is noble, true, etc. – think on these things
· Relying on the Holy Spirit

Many of the above items are discussed in this Anthology.

The Strength Target – Service

When soul, heart and mind are all aligned, it is then that we are best able to serve God in the way that He wants. But even now, Satan is still lurking to try and rob God of the fruit that He wants us to bear for Him.

Paul in his emotional, motivational speech to the Ephesian elders in the book of Acts said, somewhat surprisingly perhaps, that the Church of God was purchased with Jesus' blood. We are used to thinking of the cross-work of Christ in terms of laying down his life for his bride, or in relation to the Church the Body. But here we see that there was an additional goal which had the very same price.

Paul warned that, after his departure, savage wolves and false teaching would come in which would decimate the flock. The Church the Body in general is beyond Satan's reach, the gates of Hades shall never prevail against it. But the same is not true of the Churches of God. As much as at any time in the last 120 years perhaps, the Churches of God are under attack and, especially in the Western world, the testimony hangs by a thread in certain places. With each lampstand of testimony that is removed, the light that seeks to be faithful to God's revealed will and Word gets that bit dimmer – a testimony that Jesus died for. Each of us in Churches of God has a responsibility to establish that which remains, and more than that, with God's help, expand our borders and horizons, both numerically and spiritually.

The Strength - Enemy Strategy

·Divide and Conquer – Satan knows that the best way to cool down a fire is to separate the burning coals from each other – the same is true of Churches of God – and he can do that effectively in a number of ways.

·Dismiss the Vision – Satan can fool us into thinking that the Churches of God are insignificant or irrelevant in the world's eyes and God's eyes as well, that what it stands for is not important and we would be better off just packing it in and moving elsewhere.

·Discouragement – Satan's victories amongst the churches can be very discouraging. He may even try and convince you that God is calling you out of the Churches of God, even though God's calling is irrevocable (Romans 11:29).

The Strength - Defence Mechanism

·Shepherd care – God has put elders over each church to act as shepherds, although we can all play a part in shepherd-like care for each other. Some Churches of God lack these shepherds and we need to pray that God will raise them up.

·Bearing one another's burdens – in addition to helping each other be accountable, there is also an important practical dimension which involves helping each other out. It may be in a domestic sphere (for example assisting someone who cares full-time for an aging parent) or in the church context (such as helping run a youth club). Each of us has been given spiritual gifts, and natural abilities which can be used somewhere, someplace for God's service. We need to find out what that service is and throw ourselves into it!

·Leave no man (or woman) behind! – each one of us knows people who used to be members of Churches of God but, for a variety of reasons, no longer are. God has the power to bring them back and we might be able to play a part in that. In addition, we need to be vigilant to identify those who are struggling, again for a variety of possible reasons, and draw alongside them to provide a listening ear and wise counsel.

·Looking upwards and looking forwards – it is easy to get bogged down in the weeds and the frustrations of everyday life, but we need to be reminded constantly of the big picture – of what we have been called into and ultimately where we are heading.

Stand up, Stand Up for Jesus

Stand up, stand up for Jesus, ye soldiers of the cross;
Lift high His royal banner, it must not suffer loss.
From victory unto victory His army shall He lead,
Till every foe is vanquished, and Christ is Lord indeed.

Stand up, stand up for Jesus, the trumpet call obey;
Forth to the mighty conflict, in this His glorious day.
Ye that are brave now serve Him against unnumbered foes;
Let courage rise with danger, and strength to strength oppose.

Stand up, stand up for Jesus, stand in His strength alone;
The arm of flesh will fail you, ye dare not trust your own.
Put on the Gospel armour, each piece put on with prayer;
Where duty calls or danger, be never wanting there.

Stand up, stand up for Jesus, each soldier to his post,
Close up the broken column, and shout through all the host:
Make good the loss so heavy, in those that still remain,
And prove to all around you that death itself is gain.

Stand up, stand up for Jesus, the strife will not be long;
This day the noise of battle, the next the victor's song.
To those who vanquish evil a crown of life shall be;
They with the King of Glory shall reign eternally.
George Duffield Jnr.

22 BATTLE ROUND 3 – SATAN V JESUS (GUY JARVIE)

"...I write to you, young men, because you are strong, and the word of God lives in you, and you have overcome the evil one" (1 John 2:14).

The temptation of Jesus by Satan reveals lots of the cunning of the evil one to us and it warns us as well of the danger of the devil's temptations in our life and service. We must overcome his temptations if we are to be effective servants of God. Temptations of the adversary come early in the Christian experience and many believers fall to rise no more. The more decisive our victories, the more effective our service will be. Compromise weakens us. It is important for us to see that, whatever the circumstances in which we are being tested, behind them all is the adversary seeking to turn us away from our confidence and faith in God.

Led by the Spirit, Jesus was forty days in the wilderness after His baptism by John; forty days of loneliness with the adversary near. At the close of those forty days He was hungry because He had taken our humanity on Himself. The adversary was quick to suggest a way to satisfy His hunger. Was He really the Son of God? Then surely He could make the stones into bread! The temptation contained two suggestions. The first cast doubt on whether He was really the Son of God; and the second, that He could surely look after Himself. He must eat to live! Jesus dismissed the first suggestion and put the second in its right place. We do not only live by bread but by the word of God. What a great truth this is and yet many people forget it!

What a powerful motive "bread" is and how effective it is in the adversary's warfare and temptations! We are busy people – we must be for we must eat to live and, as Paul told the Thessalonians, "the one who is unwilling to work shall not eat."

We must think of our work, our homes, our studies, our business, our future – all are necessary. But these, though needed, are all within the "bread" of life and we can't live, spiritually, by these alone. And so the adversary pushes the "bread" and many are deceived and fall away. We must hear the word of God and we must meditate on it for ourselves. That will mean more than just reading verses and then closing the book. We must take time to think about it and allow it to mould our lives and correct our errors. We must believe its promises and make them ours by faith.

If "bread" becomes the chief motive of our lives, then our spiritual life will ebb away and we will have no strength. Let's not let the adversary deceive us when he puts present gain in front of us at the expense of doing God's will. And so the adversary went on to his next temptation, showing Jesus all the kingdoms of the world and their glory. "It will all be yours", he said, "if ..." This was a more subtle temptation but Jesus answered the temptation from the same book – the book of Deuteronomy. If He listened to the tempter, then there need be no suffering, no loss and no cross – nothing but success! That was tempting; but not to Him who had laid aside His glory to do the Father's will. He brushed aside the tempter with the word, "Worship the Lord your God and serve him only." How often the prospect of earthly success brings believers down. The glory of this world may not seem like idolatry but let us remember from Colossians 3:5 that coveting is idolatry.

"...Some people, eager for money, have wandered from the faith and pierced themselves with many griefs" (1 Timothy 6:10). This also has its roots in coveting. Let us flee from this because the tempter is behind it and some good men and women have fallen to this temptation. When "things" take first place in our hearts, then the adversary is succeeding. When we think we can follow Christ without suffering with Him, without confessing Him to others, without losing for His sake - then the adversary is succeeding and we are being deceived.

Our age is an age of "things". Though even in this materialistic age, some turn aside to spiritism; false religions grip others, but the great majority is godless and materialistic. The worship of the living God is at stake. Does our soul thirst for Him? If not, then the adversary is succeeding and the things of men take His place. If that's the case, let us weep our way back again to Him. Let us consider everything a loss because of the surpassing worth of knowing Christ Jesus.

A third temptation still lay before the Lord - to demonstrate His power for His own glory. But pride was unknown by Him. He had seen this bring down the tempter himself and He warned His disciples of it in Luke 10:17-20. And so, "When the devil had finished all this tempting, he left him until an opportune time. Jesus returned to Galilee in the power of the Spirit..." (Luke 4:13-14). Only as we overcome the evil one can we be strong. To do that, we must be men and women who have the word of God in us. As we overcome the evil one, we become wise in praying for others and wise in soul-winning.

In his epistle, John wrote to fathers (the mature men), to young men (those strong to serve) and to little children (those growing up in Christ). His word to young men is particularly of overcoming the evil one and it is principally to the young that this chapter is addressed. See the tempter behind every temptation and meet him in the way the Master met him in confidence in the word of God. When the temptation is overcome and past you will come out to serve, as the Master did, in the power of the Spirit.

Ho, My Comrades

Ho, my comrades! See the signal waving in the sky!
Reinforcements now appearing, victory is nigh.
See the mighty host advancing, Satan leading on;
Mighty ones around us falling, courage almost gone!
See the glorious banner waving! Hear the trumpet blow!
In our Leader's Name we triumph over ev'ry foe.
Fierce and long the battle rages, but our help is near;
Onward comes our great Commander, cheer, my comrades, cheer!
"Hold the fort, for I am coming," Jesus signals still;
Wave the answer back to Heaven, "By Thy grace we will."

P.P Bliss wrote this song based on an incident from the American civil war in 1864. General Sherman's army lay camped in Atlanta – the enemy passed their right flank, gained the rear, and commenced the destruction of the railroad leading north, burning blockhouses and capturing the small garrisons along the line. Sherman's army was put in rapid motion to save 1.5 million rations at Altoona Pass, where there were just 1,500 men.

They were completely surrounded by 6,000 men and summoned to surrender. They refused and a sharp fight commenced. The defenders were slowly driven into a small fort on the crest of the hill. Many had fallen and the result seemed to render the prolonging of the fight hopeless. At this moment an officer caught sight of a white signal flag far away across the valley, twenty miles distant, upon the top of

Kenesaw Mountain. The signal was answered, and soon the message was waved across from mountain to mountain:

"Hold the fort; I am coming. W. T. Sherman."

Cheers went up; every man was nerved to a full appreciation of the position; and under a murderous fire, which killed or wounded more than half the men in the fort - they held the fort for three hours until the advance guard of Sherman's army came up. The enemy was obliged to retreat.

Battle Bible Verses 2

Matthew 15:7-8: "You hypocrites! Isaiah was right when he prophesied about you: saying 'These people honour me with their lips, but their heart is far from me.'"

Acts 7:51: "You stiff-necked people! Your hearts and ears are still uncircumcised. You are just like your ancestors: you always resist the Holy Spirit!"

Acts 11:23: "...He (Barnabas)...was glad and encouraged them all to remain true to the Lord with all their hearts."

Acts 13:22: "I have found David, son of Jesse, a man after my own heart; he will do everything I want him to do."

2 Timothy 2:25-26: "...leading them to a knowledge of the truth, and that they will come to their senses and escape from the trap of the devil, who has taken them captive to do his will."

23 ISRAEL'S BATTLE – THE AMALEKITES AND THE PHILISTINES (EDWIN STANLEY)

Glorious revelation is not a guarantee of victory

"When Moses reported this to all the Israelites, they mourned bitterly. Early the next morning they set out for the highest point in the hill country, saying, 'Now we are ready to go up to the land the LORD promised. Surely we have sinned!' But Moses said, 'Why are you disobeying the LORD's command? This will not succeed! Do not go up, because the LORD is not with you. You will be defeated by your enemies, for the Amalekites and the Canaanites will face you there. Because you have turned away from the LORD, he will not be with you and you will fall by the sword.' Nevertheless, in their presumption they went up toward the highest point in the hill country, though neither Moses nor the ark of the LORD's covenant moved from the camp. Then the Amalekites and the Canaanites who lived in that hill country came down and attacked them and beat them down all the way to Hormah" (Numbers 14:39-45).

Israel had everything going for them. They had evidence of God's presence with them, seen physically in the cloud of Glory and the pillar of Fire. They also had the Tabernacle laid out before them with an operating priest and priesthood. They had a great leader in Moses and they had evidence of the good things that were in the land God had promised for them. They also had daily supplies of manna which was a testimony to the faithfulness of the God that they followed in their journeys.

Why then did they "go off the rails"? How could they get it so horribly and fatally wrong, as they refused to believe the evidence and the witness of Caleb and Joshua, preferring instead the testimony of the other ten who failed to trust in God's promises, presence and power?Exodus 13:18 tells us that they had left Egypt equipped for battle so it was not a result of being ill-prepared. No, their problem was not in lack of evidence of God's presence and glory, nor in their equipment; rather it lay in their own hearts and minds as they doubted, feared and distrusted God - and it led to failure and defeat by the men of Amalek and Canaan.

Proverbs 29:25 says "Fear of man will prove to be a snare, but whoever trusts in the LORD is kept safe" whilst 2 Timothy 1:7-8 states "for the Spirit God gave us does not make us timid, but gives us power, love and self-discipline. So do not be ashamed of the testimony about our Lord..."

Amalek often speaks of the "flesh" whilst Canaan carries the idea of a "pedlar" or "trafficker"; both of which when coupled together give a great insight into the effects of our old nature joining forces with the standards of this world that are rooted in wealth, possessions and personal advancement rather than in a deepening and progressive spiritual enrichment from the knowledge of God.

In Churches of God today there is no lack of evidence of God's presence; new churches are being established, disciples are being made and there is a growing enthusiasm for the powerful revelation of God's House in many countries of this world. However there is still the vital necessity to hold fast to the revelation of God's promises, presence and power in our warfare too – for failure to do so will inevitably lead to the triumph of our old nature and this world and the ruin of many lives for God. Deuteronomy 4:35 says: "You were shown these things so that you might know that the LORD is God; besides him there is no other." We will do well to learn that lesson in our warfare today.

Neglect in the Lord's things brings certain defeat

"And Samuel's word came to all Israel. Now the Israelites went out to fight against the Philistines. The Israelites camped at Ebenezer, and the Philistines at Aphek. The Philistines deployed their forces to meet Israel, and as the battle spread, Israel was defeated by the Philistines, who killed about four thousand of them on the battlefield. When the soldiers returned to camp, the elders of Israel asked, 'Why did the LORD bring defeat on us today before the Philistines? Let us bring the ark of the LORD's covenant from Shiloh, so that he may go with us and save us from the hand of our enemies.'

So the people sent men to Shiloh, and they brought back the ark of the covenant of the LORD Almighty, who is enthroned between the cherubim. And Eli's two sons, Hophni and Phinehas, were there with the ark of the covenant of God. When the ark of the LORD's covenant came into the camp, all Israel raised such a great shout that the ground shook. Hearing the uproar, the Philistines asked, 'What's all this shouting in the Hebrew camp?' When they learned that the ark of the LORD had come into the camp, the Philistines were afraid. 'A god has come into the camp,' they said. 'Oh no! Nothing like this has happened before. We're doomed! Who will deliver us from the hand of these mighty gods? They are the gods who struck the Egyptians with all kinds of plagues in the wilderness. Be strong, Philistines! Be men, or you will be subject to the Hebrews, as they have been to you. Be men, and fight!'

So the Philistines fought, and the Israelites were defeated and every man fled to his tent. The slaughter was very great; Israel lost thirty thousand foot soldiers. The ark of God was captured, and Eli's two sons, Hophni and Phinehas, died" (1 Samuel 4:1-11). God had clearly told Eli that the behaviour of his sons was leading Israel to disaster, and that Hophni and Phinehas would die on the same day. Their offhanded, careless handling of the sacrifices of Israel was blasphemous in God's sight and judgement was to fall upon them. Samuel, however, was the channel for God's word during the days of Eli and his sons and he enabled Israel to rediscover their God. When the Philistines gave Israel a heavy beating, they turned to the Ark of God, bringing both it and Eli's two sons to the battlefield. Their confidence and hope was in the Ark itself, not in the God who was enthroned above it and their vain hope for deliverance was to be dashed to pieces. Their actions allowed God's enemies to triumph. It brought the Ark of the Covenant into a foreign idol's house and brought dishonour to the name of God.

Why? Because they treated the offering of the LORD with contempt. It was a long time before Israel learned to turn to God with all their heart and to serve Him alone and that came through the leadership of Samuel, who was a man of the word and of prayer. 1 Corinthians 11:27-32 shows us that our handling of the Lord's things, especially with respect to the Lord Jesus (of whom the Ark of the Covenant speaks so clearly), is a sure way of allowing the adversary freedom to bring our warfare to a shuddering halt and to bring our lovely Saviour into disrepute.

"Depart, depart, go out from there! Touch no unclean thing! Come out from it and be pure, you who carry the articles of the LORD's house. But you will not leave in haste or go in flight; for the LORD will go before you, the God of Israel will be your rear guard" (Isaiah 52:11-12).

With Colossians 2:20-23 this shows how much care we need to display in our handling of God's holy things. We must not be careless, and it is vitally important to display reverence and awe in our approach to God.

"Therefore, since we are receiving a kingdom that cannot be shaken, let us be thankful, and so worship God acceptably with reverence and awe, for our 'God is a consuming fire'" (Hebrews 12:28-29).

Israel never won a battle relying on physical things; their victories came because God worked for them, because they trusted in Him implicitly and served Him alone. Likewise our spiritual warfare does not rely on physical things. Paul teaches us that in 2 Corinthians 10:4. We learn, just as Israel did, that God's word reveals His will and that will has to be followed exactly and carefully or else we will bring Him into disrepute and heap dishonour onto the Lord Jesus. Samuel shows us that when we obediently follow exactly what we are told then God is free to work in and through us to His glory and honour.

Battle Quotes 5

"What if you have fallen for a tempting ruse of the enemy? What if you're not the most brilliant swordsman in the army? You hold "Excalibur" in your hand! Get behind the lines for a break if you're too weak to go on, and strengthen yourself with a powerful draught of the wine of Romans 8:1-4. Then get back into the fight before your muscles get stiff!" (John White)

"Our warfare is spiritual, our promised land is heaven, and our enemy is Satan and his hosts of wickedness. Are they depriving us of the full joy of what God has made available in Christ's work at Calvary? Instead of being happy, vibrant, prosperous Christians, is it possible that we are living deprived, unhappy, fearful, starved lives, because our enemy has gained the upper hand? Is this possible? Is it true?" (Reg Darke)

"Morale is vital to victory and discouragement is deadly." (John White)

24 BATTLING AGAINST...SEXUAL IMMORALITY (ALAN TOMS)

Some of you might lead relatively sheltered lives and the subject I'm going to talk about may never have presented itself to you as a problem. Others whose lives bring them into daily contact with the world find themselves confronted with a very real battle. The seriousness of it was impressed on me recently when a university graduate confided that he thought he was the only person in his block who didn't sleep around at weekends. Another young disciple battling against fierce temptation said she was considered weird by her colleagues because she refused to have sex. Peer pressure can be very strong and the scale of the battle which faces the disciple of the Lord Jesus in today's world is immense.

I make no apology for writing so plainly, for it is a battle which ought to concern all of us. If we are among the fortunate ones who do not face it personally, then let us at least get to grips with it to make it an earnest part of our constant supplication that the Lord will give all His young men and young women strength to say "No" when temptation knocks so strongly and so persistently at the door. It is with a view to helping one another to stand our ground - and to know the ground we stand on - that this chapter is written. "Water wears away stones", Job says, and there is always the danger that the constant repetition of what so many around us believe might make the disciple lower his standards. But that must never be. "You shall be holy, for I am holy" is a word which stands for all time.

It is not a new battle, of course. Immorality was prominent among the fearful sins which compelled the Lord to cleanse the earth at the time of the Flood. And, not many generations after Noah and his family walked out on to a cleansed earth, we find rampant the gross uncleanness of Sodom and Gomorrah. In New Testament times the Corinthian disciples lived in a city renowned for its promiscuity. If there is anything new in our day it is perhaps the openness with which God's word is defied and the shamelessness with which people speak of pre-marital and extra-marital sex. God says it is wrong but the world condones it and that is where the disciple of the Lord Jesus has to take his or her stand. Behind the world is the great Tempter himself who from the beginning has refuted what God has said. Isaiah's words are still applicable: "Woe to those who call evil good and good evil, who put darkness for light and light for darkness, who put bitter for sweet and sweet for bitter" (Isaiah 5:20).

It seemed sweet to Amnon when he fell in love with his half-sister Tamar and with the help of his subtle cousin devised a way to force his sister to provide the sexual pleasure he wanted. But the thing turned sour on him, and the word of God says strikingly that the hatred with which he hated her greater than the love with which he loved her. "'Stolen water is sweet; food eaten in secret is delicious!' But little do they know that the dead are there, that her guests are deep in the realm of the dead" (Proverbs 9:17-18). Solomon's words proved literally true in this case, and before the end of the chapter that is where Amnon found himself - in the realm of the dead, murdered by his own brother. The story is in 2 Samuel 13.

"But if we love one another, why shouldn't we? Isn't this God's way of expressing our love?" That is a common argument and the plain answer is that this is a God-given way whereby a man and woman express their love for one another, but only within the marriage bond. About that there is no doubt whatever. The word of God is clear: "It is

God's will that you should be sanctified: that you should avoid sexual immorality; that each of you should learn to control your own body in a way that is holy and honourable, not in passionate lust like the pagans, who do not know God; and that in this matter no one should wrong or take advantage of a brother or sister. The Lord will punish all those who commit such sins, as we told you and warned you before. For God did not call us to be impure, but to live a holy life. Therefore, anyone who rejects this instruction does not reject a human being but God, the very God who gives you his Holy Spirit" (1 Thessalonians 4:3-8).

For those who love the Lord Jesus the matter rests there. There can be no argument against the plain word of God. But some do argue, of course, sometimes even with God! "If we love one another and no-one else is affected, why shouldn't we?" is another common argument. But others are affected invariably. Sometimes children are born as a result, even in these days of easily available contraceptives - born into a home where they are not really wanted and into the insecurity of a one-parent family. And many a girl has lived to deeply regret consenting to sexual relations. "...Where could I get rid of my disgrace...?" The awful wail of David's daughter, Tamar, has been echoed by so many since. It happens under the guise of love. But it is lust, not love. True love always seeks what is best for the one loved. "Love is patient, love is kind...it does not dishonour others, it is not self-seeking..." Without a doubt it is best to wait for God's time and to enjoy His gifts when He gives them and not before.

Anyone who genuinely seeks help in their battle should carefully think about the arguments advanced by the apostle Paul in 1 Corinthians 6:12-20. If possible it is helpful to read the portion in different versions beside the one you normally use and allow its message to sink into your minds. Notice three strong reasons why we should "flee sexual immorality", that is, remove ourselves as quickly as possible from any situation where temptation might strongly present itself. That is what

Joseph did when he fled from his master's wife. He lost his coat and he lost his job that day, but he won the battle and kept a clear conscience - that is what matters above everything else. "...How then could I do such a wicked thing and sin against God?" he asked. There was no lowering of standards for Joseph. He recognized it for what it was - great wickedness and sin against God. And three reasons why it is such serious sin are advanced by the apostle Paul in this portion of scripture:

•"the body is ...for the Lord; and the Lord for the body." And that applies not only in our present life but in eternity as well. God has put two strong appetites into the human body, one for food and the other for sex. Both are necessary for the normal functioning of life on earth, but each in its place. Both have to be controlled; and both will be done away when life on earth is over. But not so our bodies, for they are redeemed, and when the Lord Jesus returns they will be changed to become like His own glorious body. We must always remember that God has a purpose for our bodies beyond the present one.

•Our bodies are members of Christ, joined to Him in that glorious mystical union called the Church His Body. When the full implication of this truth grips the heart, we realize how inappropriate it is for a believer to be joined in sexual union with anyone other than his or her God-given spouse.

•"Do you not know that your bodies are temples of the Holy Spirit, who is in you, whom you have received from God? You are not your own; you were bought at a price." We do know it and so did the Corinthians but sometimes we forget and the wonder of it fails to grip our hearts. But the fact remains that one of the Persons of the Godhead has taken up residence in our bodies. We have been purchased by the precious blood of Christ and sealed unto the day of redemption by the indwelling Holy Spirit and we are not our own. We have no right therefore to decide our own code of conduct. We belong to the One who has purchased us.

So the apostle Paul closes with those memorable words, "Glorify God therefore in your body" (RV). This is life's highest purpose. "I have glorified You on the earth," (RV) said God's perfect Servant of His life of service. Let us each make it the all-absorbing object of our lives, to glorify God in thought and word and action, and when we appear before Christ's judgement seat we shall be thankful indeed.

The A-Z of Satan – Q to Z

- Roaring lion – "Be alert and of sober mind. Your enemy the devil prowls around like a roaring lion looking for someone to devour" (1 Peter 5:8).
- Ruler of the darkness – "For we do not wrestle against flesh and blood, but against principalities, against powers, against the rulers of the darkness of this age, against spiritual hosts of wickedness in the heavenly places" (Ephesians 6:12 NKJV).
- Ruler of demons – "But some of them said, 'He casts out demons by Beelzebub, the ruler of the demons'" (Luke 11:15 NKJV).
- Ruler of this world – "Now is the judgement of this world; now the ruler of this world will be cast out" (John 12:31 NKJV).
- Satan – "and He was in the wilderness forty days, being tempted by Satan. He was with the wild animals..." (Mark 1:13).
- Serpent of old – "So the great dragon was cast out, that serpent of old, called the Devil and Satan, who deceives the whole world; he was cast to the earth..." (Revelation 12:9 NKJV).
- Star – "The fifth angel sounded his trumpet, and I saw a star that had fallen from the sky to the earth. The star was given the key to the shaft of the Abyss" (Revelation 9:1)
- Tempter – "The tempter came to Him and said, 'If you are the Son of God, tell these stones to become bread'" (Matthew 4:3).
- Thief – "The thief comes only to steal and kill and destroy; I have come that they may have life and have it to the full" (John 10:10).
- Wicked one – "above all, taking the shield of faith with which

you will be able to quench all the fiery darts of the wicked one" (Ephesians 6:16 NKJV).